'68 at 40 Retrospective

By Steve Binder

Featuring unpublished photos from the private collections of Robert Brower and Timothy Mulrenan

JAT Productions/Chicago/USA

SINGER presents....

ELVIS!

NBC-TV / DEC.3 / 9 PM (EST)

P. O. Box 56372, Chicago, IL 60656-0372

Acknowledgments:

Jeff Abraham, Ted Bigger, Steve Binder, Robert Brower, Mike Eder, John Heath, John Michael Heath, Gene McAvoy, Tim Mulrenan, John Szymanski, Doreen Tunzi, Kristina Tunzi

Robert Brower:

I would like to thank Steve Binder and Jeff Abraham for taking my call and for their dedication and time. Thank you Joe Tunzi for your tireless work and guidance. To my friends and family – my grandmother Evelyn, my mother Marie, Danielle, my daughter, Sunny, Craig and Ross. To Roberto and Tim for giving me this opportunity, thanks. Special thanks to my father for introducing me to photography when I was a child. Hope you enjoy these incredible images!

Timothy Mulrenan:

When these images of Elvis were scanned and shown to me, I could not believe the clarity of them. I knew then that this was something the Public needed to see. I would like to thank Steve Binder, Jeff Abraham and Joe Tunzi for making it all possible. To Robert Brower for bringing these images to life. To Roberto for bringing these images to my attention. To my wife Marian and my Family for believing in me. Thank you. Hope you enjoy!

For all inquires about the photos in this book please visit:
www.elvispresleyphotos.com

Thanks to Jerry Schilling, Greil Marcus, Alex Coletti, and Colin Escott.

A special thank you to Priscilla Presley.

All black and white photography, documents and original notes courtesy of Steve Binder. Original notes appear in Steve's own hand writing.

Photos on page 121 courtesy of Kevin Parry/The Paley Center for Media

All sketches on page iv courtesy and copy written by © Gene McAvoy

Book Layout/Design: Tressa Foster

A Joseph A. Tunzi Publication
Library of Congress Control Number
2008930558 / Hardcover
ISBN Number 9781888464191
Printed in Canada
Visit us on the web at
www.jatpublishing.com

Contents

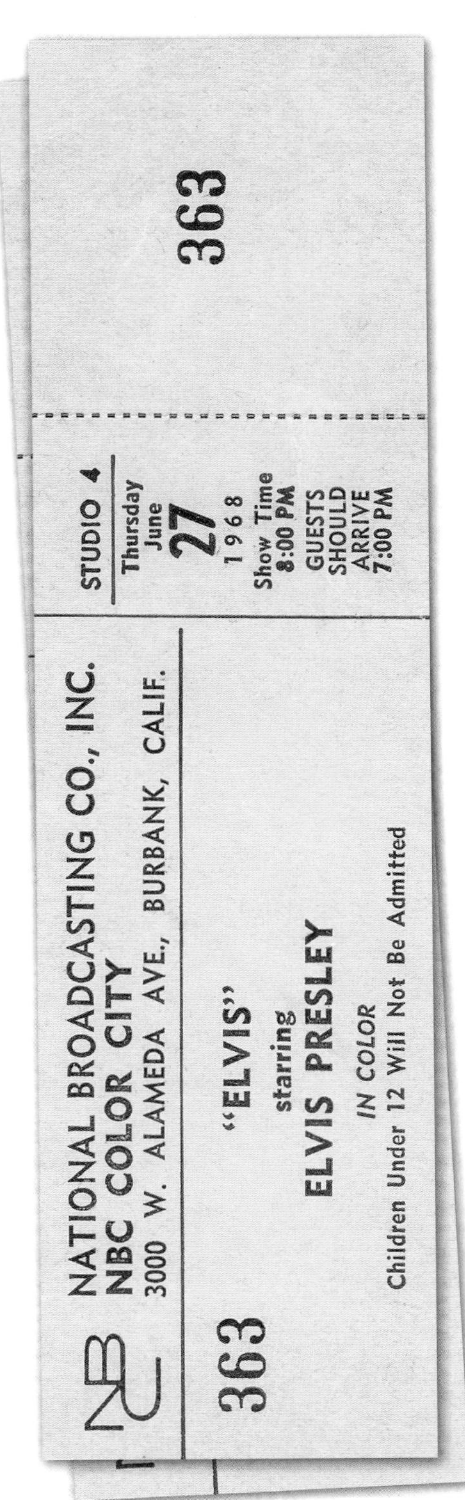
363
STUDIO 4
Thursday
June
27
1968
Show Time
8:00 PM
GUESTS
SHOULD
ARRIVE
7:00 PM
NATIONAL BROADCASTING CO., INC.
NBC COLOR CITY
3000 W. ALAMEDA AVE., BURBANK, CALIF.
"ELVIS"
starring
ELVIS PRESLEY
IN COLOR
Children Under 12 Will Not Be Admitted
363

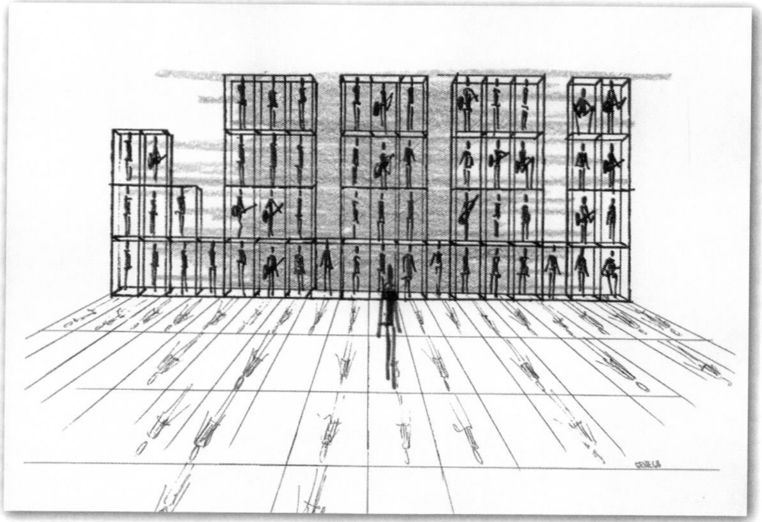

Sketches of the set design by Art Director, Gene McAvoy.

Preface

"MEMORIES, PRESSED BETWEEN THE PAGES OF MY MIND MEMORIES, SWEETENED THROUGH THE AGES JUST LIKE WINE."

TWO SIMPLE LINES FROM THE SONG LYRIC TO "MEMORIES" WRITTEN BY BILLY STRANGE AND MAC DAVIS AND SUNG BY ELVIS PRESLEY ON HIS 1968 NBC TELEVISION SPECIAL, SIMPLY TITLED, "ELVIS."

HAS IT BEEN 40 YEARS? IT SEEMS LIKE ONLY YESTERDAY A GROUP OF CREATIVE YOUNG MEN GOT TOGETHER WITH THE KING TO CREATE MEMORIES THAT WOULD LAST US ALL A LIFETIME.

I DEDICATE THIS BOOK TO ALL THOSE WHO I HAD THE PRIVILEGE OF SHARING THEIR CREATIVE IDEAS WITH IN WHAT IS NOW REFERRED TO AS "THE ELVIS PRESLEY COMEBACK SPECIAL."

I AM HAPPY TO SAY I STILL CALL THEM ALL "MY FRIENDS." THANK YOU: CHRIS BEARDE, BILL BELEW, EARL BROWN, ALLAN BLYE, BOB FINKEL, BILLY GOLDENBERG, GENE McAVOY, BONES HOWE, JAIME ROGERS, TOM SARNOFF, CLAUDE THOMPSON AND ALL THE TALENTED MEN AND WOMEN WHO PARTICIPATED IN ONE OF THE GREATEST EVENTS IN TELEVISION HISTORY.

LONG LIVE THE KING OF ROCK 'N' ROLL.

STEVE BINDER

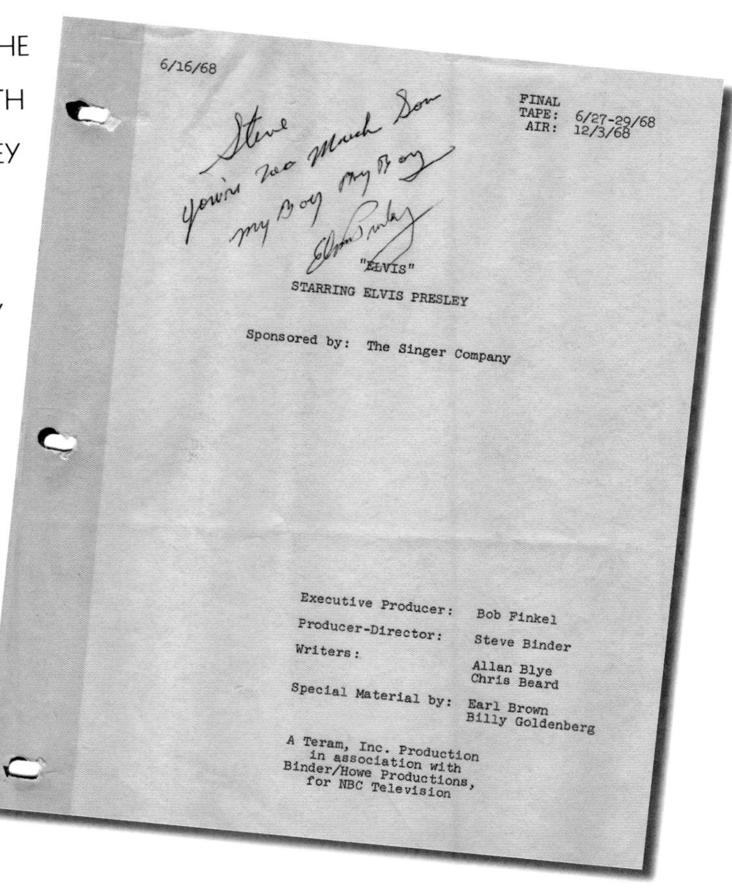

6/16/68

FINAL
TAPE: 6/27-29/68
AIR: 12/3/68

"ELVIS"
STARRING ELVIS PRESLEY

Sponsored by: The Singer Company

Executive Producer: Bob Finkel
Producer-Director: Steve Binder
Writers: Allan Blye
Chris Beard
Special Material by: Earl Brown
Billy Goldenberg

A Teram, Inc. Production
in association with
Binder/Howe Productions,
for NBC Television

DAILY VARIETY DAILY

Vol. 138 No. 30 Hollywood, California - 90028, Thursday, Jan. 18, 1968 Ten Cents

PRESLEY'S 2-PLY DEAL WITH NBC

January 31, 1968

Dear Mr. Finkel:

The Colonel asked us to send these along to you.

Col. Parker's Office

(Bio's, 45 records, tape + LP catalogues, pix, Cadillac brochure; kept bios + 2 pix)

Chapter 1

Pre-Special

Without a doubt, the most publicly important show that I ever produced and directed was the 1968 Elvis Presley NBC special, "ELVIS." Now I know that there are dozens of books, blogs and movies written and made about the special, and I've even given interviews to some of the authors. But now, it's time to tell my story about "ELVIS."

On April 9th 1968 the TV special "Petula" premiered and a few days later, a call came into my office from television producer Bob Finkel. Finkel explained to me that he had read about the famous "touch' on the "Petula" NBC special where the singer briefly touched Harry Belafonte's arm during a duet and how after heavy pressure from the advertising sponsor, I had refused to remove it from the special. It was the first time in a variety show that a white and black performer touched one another on national television.

As I remember our conversation, Finkel thought the controversy surrounding the special and my being a young 'rebel' would make me a perfect fit for Elvis Presley. He explained to me that some time ago Tom Sarnoff, the West Coast Vice President of NBC, had run into Colonel Tom Parker, Elvis' legendary manager at a social event, and the two had worked out a deal for NBC to broadcast a television special and as part of the overall deal finance a feature film starring Elvis sometime in the future. The movie was "Change of Habit."

Finkel told me he was going to be the executive producer of the special but was not sure it would ever really get made because Elvis was balking at doing television. He was concerned that when he met Elvis on a few occasions, he was politely addressed as "Mr. Finkel" instead of Bob and therefore felt Elvis needed to relate to someone closer to his own age. I told him that I'd think about it and get back to him.

I discussed the opportunity with my partner, successful record producer, Bones Howe, who told me I'd be crazy to turn down a chance to work with Elvis. Bones had engineered a couple of Elvis' sessions and thought that Elvis and I would make a great combination. I phoned Finkel back and told him that if a meeting could be arranged with Elvis alone and if we hit it off, I would make the commitment. I was at the time seriously considering leaving television altogether and focusing my career on directing feature films with a firm offer for a film from legendary movie producer Walter Wanger.

Soon after my phone conversation with Finkel, Bones and I met Bob for lunch at the Brown Derby restaurant in Hollywood for the first time so we could get to know one another and talk about the possibility of working together. I liked Finkel immediately having followed his career for years, as he represented a generation of respected variety producer/directors before guys like me even entered the field. But after our lunch meeting, I never heard back from him so after a few days went by I contacted Bob to find out what was going on. He sent me the following letter on April 16th:

"Dear Steve: As I told you during our last meeting, as soon as the Colonel clears the dates of the last two weeks of May and the first two weeks of June, we will be able to then sit down with Tom Sarnoff and work out our deal. I just spoke to the Colonel; and, there are certain contractual points being worked out between NBC and Elvis Presley which are holding up the clearance of these dates. But, I am being assured by all, that this will be decided very shortly. Thanks again for your interest. I am very happy at the prospect of us working together; and, I am sure it will be a gigantic and tremendously exciting project. Cordially, (signed) Bob Finkel.

Soon after, I received a phone call from Finkel telling me that he was prepared to hire me and he would like Bones and me to meet him at his NBC offices in Burbank. After a brief conversation and walk to the NBC stages where Finkel was producing the "Jerry Lewis Show," we agreed to move forward. He told us that he would arrange a meeting with the Colonel as soon as possible and we left with a good feeling about working together.

On May 7th, Finkel sent me all the Elvis material that Parker sent to his office back on January 31st, so I could prepare myself for our meeting with both the Colonel and eventually Elvis.

Elvis fans already know that the Colonel, when making the deal with NBC, insisted that the program be a Christmas show with Elvis merely saying "Hello," "Merry Christmas" and "Goodnight" in between singing twenty-six Christmas songs. NBC didn't care what the show was as long as they got Elvis on the air and went out to find a sponsor who would pick up the tab for the show. Their sales department already had a sponsor relationship with Farlan Myers at J. Walter Thompson Advertising Company who represented Singer Sewing Machines and as a favor to them practically gave them the Elvis special as part of package deal. Singer also bought two more specials that year that aired on NBC, "Don Ho" from Hawaii and flamboyant pianist "Liberace." Kentucky Fried Chicken and Mrs. Paul's tried desperately to sponsor the Elvis show and probably would have doubled or tripled the price that Singer actually paid for it.

Finkel arranged for Bones and myself to meet with Colonel Parker at his office at the MGM studios in Culver City. The meeting took place very early in the morning on May 10th. Colonel Parker's office looked like a large kitchen you'd find in a Tennessee home with a large table in the center of the room covered by an oilcloth with oak chairs surrounding it. Sitting on some high bar stools in back of the room, Tom Diskin, the Colonel's right hand man, and Freddy Bienstock, of Hill and Range Music, were there to greet us as well.

For the next thirty minutes, the Colonel did all the talking, and started the conversation with his dancing chicken story. He told us about the time he was working in a carnival and his act was getting people to buy tickets to see his dancing chickens. He told us that he had about seven chickens and a hot plate covered with straw and when he plugged the electrical cord into the socket with "Turkey In The Straw" playing loudly on the speakers, the chickens would start jumping up and down from the burning heat of the hot plate. I thought it was extremely cruel and definitely not funny.

Next, the Colonel showed us a copy of Elvis' contract with MGM. He bragged about his one-page standard contract that he had with all the film studios whenever Elvis made a movie. It stated how many days Elvis would be required to film and what time he would start work and what time he could leave each day. He pointed out to us that the most important clause was the one million dollar fee for Elvis' services. The Colonel told us that once the payment was made Elvis would do anything you asked of him as long as it was in the contract.

The Colonel obviously wanted to impress us with his astute business sense. In my layman opinion it was a terrible contract. It did not require the studios to give Elvis any ownership in his movies, nor were there any provisions for ancillary rights that could have added up to millions of dollars for Elvis's future. Worse yet, Elvis would sing any song that the writer of the screenplay put into the script. Most had never written a song in their life let alone a rock 'n' roll song for Elvis.

Near the end of the meeting the Colonel handed me two gifts. One was a box with Elvis' face on the front cover surrounded by snow-capped mountains with pine trees protruding. Inside the box was a color brochure with Elvis holding the back of a cane chair and dressed in a red Eisenhower jacket, white shirt and black pants with the title "Season's Greetings from Elvis." On the back of the brochure it read "The complete script for Elvis' Special Christmas Program scheduled on your station for Sunday, December 3, 1967."

The script inside contained a breakdown of all the Christmas songs Elvis would sing: ending with "I'll Be Home For Christmas." Elvis finally spoke for a grand total of five seconds on the entire reel-to-reel 7 ½" audiotape and he was introduced by the tapes announcer Buzz Benson, whose introduction to Elvis lasted 40-seconds. His introduction to Elvis included promoting RCA Victor records of Elvis' Christmas album and the motion picture "Clambake." This box was the Colonel's Christmas gift to an estimated 4,000 local disc jockeys at radio stations across America. As the Colonel handed me the box, he told me that what was in this box was going to be the NBC "Elvis Christmas Special." There was no question in my mind that the Colonel meant every word that he said.

The next gift handed to me was a membership card and booklet to his "Snowman's Club" with the inscription, "To: Snower Steve Binder" and signed simply "Potentate." The Colonel went on to explain that to be a member in the club you had to be a great bullshitter. I accepted the cards and booklet, but hoped he realized I wasn't worthy of the 'honor'.

It was a pleasant enough meeting like at the start of a poker game where everybody at the card table is sizing up his opponent before the game begins and I kept studying the Colonel studying me. When the meeting was over, the Colonel promised to set up a meeting with Elvis later that afternoon.

Our first meeting with Elvis took place at the Binder-Howe offices located at 8833 Sunset Blvd. in Suite 410, on the Sunset Strip. Elvis, looking amazing, arrived at the pre-arranged time of four in the afternoon accompanied by Joe Esposito, Charlie Hodge, Lamar Fike and Alan Fortas. Colonel Parker showed up later by himself. The entourage sat outside in the reception area while Elvis, Bones, and I went behind closed doors. Elvis referred to me immediately by my first name. When Finkel heard about that he knew he had made the right decision.

One of my first concerns before meeting Elvis was that I wasn't sure he was living in the present. His movies had dried up and he hadn't had a hit record on the music charts for at least two or three years. We chatted for about an hour. Elvis asked me where I thought his career was at now, and I told him jokingly "In the toilet." I think he immediately respected my blunt honesty. He told me about his reluctance to do a television special because he hadn't appeared in front of a live audience for years, and he wasn't sure they'd even accept him now. I told him that there would be a big risk involved. If the special tanked, he would still be remembered as an old rock 'n' roll star of the 50's who had a fantastic career and a great personal manager, but essentially his career would be finished. On the other hand, IF the special were a success, he'd instantly re-establish himself as the King of Rock 'n' Roll in present time. I remember specifically asking him if Jimmy Webb had written the song "MacArthur Park" (a hit record at the time) for him instead of actor Richard Harris, would he have recorded it? Without hesitation he answered a definitive…"Yes." I knew then I wasn't dealing with a has-been.

I asked Elvis what he thought of today's music and the different rock bands and he said he liked some of the music and thought some of the new rock bands were great, specifically mentioning the Beatles. He went on talking unhappily about his past television experiences and how he felt they were out of his comfort zone because the only 'turf' he felt comfortable in was a recording studio. I knew what he was talking about because I felt that he was treated by many in the industry as a 'novelty act' instead of a serious performer. Steve Allen had him dress in a tuxedo with a live Beagle in front of him while he sang "Hound Dog" and Milton Berle made fun of him on his slapstick variety show. On "The Ed Sullivan Show," CBS feared that his gyrations would somehow corrupt the youth of America so they instructed the director to only shoot Elvis from the waist up. Ironically, this turned out to be a blessing in disguise for Colonel Parker and his Elvis publicity machine.

SNOWMENS LEAGUE OF AMERICA LTD.

Our Motto "Let it Snow, Let it Snow, Let it Snow!"

Address Behind Snow Man

from the desk of
HIGH POTENTATE
COL. THOMAS A. PARKER
(Snow Jobs For All Occasions)

SNOW BALLS

Free Advice at Reasonable Rates

Available from Col. Parkers Pastures...
Shetland Ponies, Ducks, Chickens, Frogs, Goats, Milk, Hams & Bacon.

also...

Limited quantaties of...

Choice Mosquito Manure

Trained Fleas

Housebroken Cockroaches

Unactive Radio Activity

Surplus War Surplus

One Red Fire Hydrant

Send for Our Free Catalog
C.O.D's Only

SNOWMEN'S LEAGUE Of America

Chief Potentate COLONEL TOM PARKER

Confidential Report Dealing with Advanced Techniques of Member Snowers

SNOW

More SNOW

DON'T PUT IT IN WRITING... PUT IT IN INVISIBLE INK.

To: Snower STEVE BINDER

There is nothing I can give you which you have not
But there is much while I cannot give you you can take.

—FRA. GIOVANNI

DATE: May 15-68

Potentate

HIGH POTENTATE COL. TOM PARKER

SNOWMENS LEAGUE OF AMERICA LTD.

This will certify that STEVE BINDER

is a Genuine Snower in good standing. This card can be signed only by the First High Potentate, and there is a chance it isn't good even then.

Nº XXXX
This Year

Potentate

FIRST HIGH POTENTATE SNOWER

First High Potentate Snower

FULL TRACK 7½ I.P.S.

ELVIS PRESLEY
SPECIAL CHRISTMAS PROGRAM

SEQUENCE

INTRO: "HERE COMES SANTA CLAUS"
ANNOUNCER
"HERE COMES SANTA CLAUS"
ANNOUNCER
"BLUE CHRISTMAS"
ANNOUNCER
"O LITTLE TOWN OF BETHLEHEM"
ANNOUNCER
MR. ROBERTSON
ANNOUNCER
"SILENT NIGHT"
"I'LL BE HOME FOR CHRISTMAS"
ANNOUNCER
"I BELIEVE"
ANNOUNCER
"IF EVERY DAY WAS LIKE CHRISTMAS"
ANNOUNCER
ANNOUNCER
"HOW GREAT THOU ART"
"HIS HAND IN MINE"
ANNOUNCER
BACKGROUND MUSIC "I'LL BE HOME FOR CHRISTMAS"
ANNOUNCER
(PICTURE RELEASE)
ELVIS: SPECIAL ELVIS MESSAGE
"I'LL BE HOME FOR CHRISTMAS"
ANNOUNCER
LOCAL MESSAGE

(5 SECONDS)
(27 SECONDS)
(2 MINUTES)
(23 SECONDS)
(2 MIN. 5 SEC.)
(13 SECONDS)
(2 MIN. 34 SEC.)
(5 SECONDS)
(1 MIN. 13 SEC.)
(12 SECONDS)
(2 MIN. 23 SEC.)
(1 MIN. 39 SEC.)
(20 SECONDS)
(2 MIN. 4 SEC.)
(12 SECONDS)
(2 MIN. 51 SEC.)
(30 SECONDS)
(16 SECONDS)
(2 MIN. 58 SEC.)
(3 MINUTES)
(19 SECONDS)
(17 SECONDS)
(40 SECONDS)
(5 SECONDS)
(1 MIN. 34 SEC.)
(7 SECONDS)
(1 MINUTE)

A complete script for Elvis' Special Christmas Program scheduled on your station for Sunday, December 3, 1967 is enclosed.

SEASON'S GREETINGS FROM ELVIS

The complete script for Elvis' Special Christmas Program scheduled on your station for Sunday, December 3, 1967.

"We had to tell people that Elvis was human and that he had something to say."
— STEVE BINDER, Producer & Director

After listening to Elvis's fears about television, I told him that I thought if we worked together he could focus on making records while I would put pictures to his music. I also told Elvis we would approach his special like a tailor making a tailor-made suit for a special customer. Because it was tailor-made for him personally, the 'suit' wouldn't fit any other person. If Elvis felt that the special we created for him wasn't right for him we'd be forced to throw the whole special out. Nobody else BUT Elvis would be able to do it.

Before he left the office, I reiterated to Elvis that I had no intentions of doing a Christmas special. I said to him, let Andy Williams or Perry Como do that. I said to Elvis if he liked where we were going, we'd continue talking and if not, we could say it was nice meeting each other. As an after thought I asked him if there was anyone that he had to have on the show other than my staff , assuming we moved forward and he asked me to include his music conductor and arranger, Billy Strange.

We agreed to meet again after my 'team' had formulated our ideas and we would present them to him. If he liked our ideas, we would move forward. If not, we would have at least had the opportunity to meet one another and be friends.

As soon as Elvis left our offices, I started to put together my 'family' to create a think-tank of people so we could come up with a concept for our next meeting with Elvis that took place a few days before he took off for Hawaii. Ann McClelland who was Bones's secretary before we formed our partnership was assigned to take notes during these meetings. In these meetings we were all equals with no pecking order based on our titles or salaries. We just sat there and we just all pitched ideas equally or tried to embellish ideas from others. To this day I love working that way surrounded by talented individuals speaking their minds freely.

Rather than describe those beginning Elvis days in my own words, here are the original Anne McClelland notes taken on May 14th and 15th as we began our discussions with Allan Blye, Chris Bearde, Earl Brown, Bill Belew and Gene McAvoy.

MAY 14 & 15 PRESLEY MEETINGS AT BINDER-HOWE

Pre-production with staff to begin immediately: Meetings with Elvis to begin on June 3rd. He will be available five days a week after 1:00PM. Aim for start of pre-record on June 15 at Western Recording Studios, taping last week of June - 2 to 4 days.

Musical material: One Christmas song, one sacred song, 4-6 new songs, remaining to be pop, rhythm & blues, country & western, gospel, etc. Some songs from Presley's movies cannot be used. Pre-record everything that really needs an Elvis sound and anything that can't be done as well at NBC. Everything that is pre-recorded will be done as though a commercial recording session.

Have an original theme written for the show to use with titles at beginning and end. Use news films and still photos as a montage of Presley's history over the theme and titles.

First 9 or 10-minutes a blockbuster performance of only Elvis. One idea is to begin with a moving gospel-rock segment. It would be a challenge to try to top it with the rest of the show. Different segments could be broken down into R&B, C&W, gospel, pop, talking, love, sports with music, etc.

Don't dwell on the past. The excitement is what is happening now. Elvis would like to say what he feels about the music of today and the future. Blend between songs with some dialogue. He needs an intimate or segment where the audience sees that he is a real person that is warm and sincere. Idea of an interview between Elvis and Leonard Bernstein.

If show is broken into segments of different types of music, each segment could contain songs from Presley's start and progress into today and songs of the future in that particular field (i.e., R&B, C&W, etc.) Bring nostalgia; freshness and a new look in each segment.

Open another segment or two that goes beyond music. Things Presley is interested in that could be related to music and segments; automobiles, motorcycles, karate, football, horses, possible correlation between Presley and electricity.

Karate dance by Jaime Rogers where Presley isn't directly involved. May use up to four different choreographers in the special for different feelings in each segment.

Wardrobe: Bill Belew should submit several sketches to Presley of different types of clothes

EXPENSES INCURRED BY BINDER/HOWE PRODUCTIONS RELATING TO THE ELVIS PRESLEY SPECIAL FROM MAY 10 - JUNE 6, 1968:

MAY 10	SUPPLIES FOR MEETING WITH ELVIS PRESLEY & AIDES: SOFT DRINKS, CUPS, NAPKINS, CIGARS, POTATO CHIPS	$ 4.36
MAY 13	SUPPLIES FOR MEETING WITH WRITERS, EXEC PRODUCER & PRODUCTION STAFF: COFFEE, CREAM, SUGAR, SPOONS ...	$ 2.38
MAY 15	SUPPLIES FOR MEETING WITH WRITERS: SOFT DRINKS	$ 1.04
MAY 16	SUPPLIES FOR MEETING WITH WRITERS & PRODUCTION STAFF: CRACKERS, CHEESE, NAPKINS, APPLE CIDER, CANDY	$ 3.88
MAY 20	SUPPLIES FOR MEETING WITH WRITERS, EXEC PRODUCER, PRODUCTION STAFF: SOFT DRINKS, COFFEE, SUGAR, COCOA, SPOONS	$ 3.61
MAY 21	SUPPLIES FOR MEETING WITH WRITERS & PRODUCTION STAFF: SOFT DRINKS, CRACKERS, CHEESE, CANDY, YOGURT, CUPS	$ 5.26
MAY 24	SUPPLIES FOR MEETING WITH WRITERS: SOFT DRINKS	$ 1.22
MAY 30	LUNCHES DURING MEETING FOR PRODUCER, P.A., ART DIRECTOR, PRODUCTION SECRETARY	$11.49

Elvis signed off to our new concept for the special at our 2nd meeting at the Binder-Howe offices shortly before he took off for Hawaii and I had invited Allan Blye and his new writing partner Chris Bearde to join us. I asked Elvis if we should wait for the Colonel to show up before talking about the show. Elvis explained that it was strictly a business arrangement, and the Colonel seldom accompanied him anywhere unless the press was present. The Colonel verified this later by telling me that he prided himself for never having spent a social evening with Elvis or even set foot in Elvis' home for a meal.

Allan and Chris begin pitching their outline for the special. And the way they came up with the idea for the special was they went out and bought every single album and 45-record that Elvis ever recorded, then locked themselves in a room and didn't leave it until they figured out the basic spine for the special. One of their most important contributions to the special was using the song "Guitar Man" to connect the various scenes that made up the story of country boy on a quest for fame and fortune.

Both of the writers, but especially Chris, have tremendous personalities and practically performed the show for Elvis. I could tell by observing Elvis's facial and body reaction that he was eating it up and loved every word that Allan and Chris were saying. In fact, when they concluded their last word, Elvis was so enthusiastic that it made me a little nervous that he didn't contest or want us to change anything.

What I've tried to accomplish with all of my specials is to move the audience in the same way that a great dramatic film tells a personal story that we can easily identify ourselves in, with the same experiences and feelings as the characters in the movie. I told Elvis that if we did this special right, it wasn't going to be just a lot of songs put together with pretty scenery and colorful costumes but subliminally tell your personal journey through life. At the end of the day, the viewer would really feel they knew him as a compassionate and loving person rather than the entertainer image they've been told by others.

"I love it," he said. "Let's do it!" Fade up on an extreme close-up of Elvis. He looks directly into the camera lens and sings: "If you're looking for trouble, you've come to the right place!" 'Trouble' would become the secret word throughout the taping.

On May 15th, I sent a letter to Norman Morrel, who worked for Bob Finkel and was handling the budget for the special asking for the following people to be confirmed: Special lyrics/Vocal arrangements: Earl Brown for $2750.00, Set designer: Gene McAvoy for $5000.00 and Costumes: Bill Belew for $2500.00.

Our creative meetings continued while Elvis vacationed in Hawaii:

MAY 20 "JUST ELVIS" MEETING AT BINDER-HOWE

Possible openings: credits with "Guitar Man" as theme. Start with soft ballad with Presley on a bare stage with stool and guitar as visible props. Begin with overture of Presley's hits with only 3 or 4 lines of each. Start with Presley singing some strong material.

Build the show keeping in mind the idea of a nightclub act where Presley performs and also communicates in some way with his studio and television audience.

Possibly 3 choreographers, one for spiritual segment, one for rock and roll and one for karate dance number. Dancers should be auditioned soon.

Spiritual segment: Rocking Negro gospel feeling. Use of dancers. Should be strong visual segment, universal religious feeling. Begin with a good solid beat that continually builds.

Country and Western Segment: Should have a good graphic look. Futuristic barn maybe with dancers as extras sitting on rafters. Western clothes with style. Might be workable as concert segment.

Rock and roll segment: Use of dancers. Audience in-the-round.

Find a situation where Presley can meet with some of the people that influenced him, such as Johnny Cash, Jerry Lee Lewis, etc. Could be worked into C&W segment.

Every other segment might be in a theater-in-the-round with the last song of each segment leading into the next segment which is in a different setting.

Possible songs for show:

1. *Hound Dog*
2. *Don't Be Cruel*
3. *Love Me Tender*
4. *All Shook Up*
5. *Jailhouse Rock*
6. *Too Much*
7. *Loving You*
8. *Teddy Bear*
9. *Are You Lonesome Tonight*
10. *Heartbreak Hotel*
11. *One Night*
12. *Return To Sender*
13. *A Little Less Conversation*
14. *Guitar Man*
15. *U.S. Male*
16. *Blue Suede Shoes*
17. *Fever*
18. *Can't Help Falling In Love*
19. *Little Sister*
20. *I'll Be Home For Christmas*
21. *I Believe*
22. *How Great Thou Art*
23. *Love Me*

"JUST ELVIS" MEETING NOTES- MAY 21 AT BINDER-HOWE

The title for the special would be "JUST ELVIS"

***Billboards:** Singer titles come in cold off of the NBC logo with their billboard (i.e., "The following program "JUST ELVIS" is brought to you by Singer") then go straight into cold opening.*

***Cold Opening:** "Guitar Man" as theme. Fill the studio with 100-200 guys dressed in black, looking like Elvis. Use mirrors. Elvis, in the midst of this black carpet of guys, dressed in white, all with guitars. The guys are in frozen position when Presley is shown, then they move with him about every 8-bars of music. The set is black, white and red with diagonal platforms or bridges going in different directions. Following "Guitar Man" is an original composition with Presley moving (using edit-tick,) then freeze picture, "Just Elvis" and fade to black.*

Commercial

(Segment ideas - not necessarily in show sequence)

***Concert Segment:** Open tight on Presley singing a ballad such as "Love Me Tender." Tape that performance twice. Once with audience (500 girls) and once without and cut in audience take at the end of the song nothing new or unusual. Let him move and groove with medleys of his hits interspersed with dialogue. Theater-in-the-round. A simple set, different than used in the opening. Presley should be alone with only a minimum of props.*

Commercial:

Mean and Evil segment: Use songs like "Trouble" from King Creole. Incorporate Karate dance. Work out a simple story line that would run through the segment. An overall "Slaughter on Tenth Avenue" feeling. Production segment with strong musical feeling and well choreographed.

Commercial:

Sentimental and Spiritual segment: Possibly incorporate one Christmas song and love songs that could lead into spiritual. Dramatic, moving, choreographed, dialogue. Spiritual universal religious feeling. Rocking Negro gospel feeling. Solid beat that continually builds. Hand clapping, foot stomping. Baptist feel. Strong visual segment with swampland or "Porgy & Bess" type sets. Possibly tape this entire segment 3-days in succession with different audiences (along with any other live segments) and edit best sections.

Commercial:

Misc. segments with country & western, rock-a-billy, rhythm & blues, rock & roll. We will have up to 6-new songs to use, depending on what is needed.

With everyone on board, it was time for Binder-Howe to close our deal with NBC. Even though the entire production was owned by NBC, Bob Finkel's company, Teram, Inc. had an exclusive contract with the network to produce shows for them. Our contract was with Finkel's company Teram, Inc., representing Elvis, and Binder-Howe Productions. The William Morris Agency's legal department prepared the contract between Teram, and our company.

5/27/68

"JUST ELVIS"

TAPE 6/26/68-6/29/68
AIR 12/3/68

RUNDOWN

---

1. Disclaimer

2. NBC Peacock

3. Commercial Billboard ????

4. xxx Cold Opening

   a. Elvis talks about his special

   b. Elvis Impersonators - Japanese, German, African, etc.

   c. "GUITAR MAN" Opening - Elvis, One Hundred Men (all looking like Elvis)

5. FIRST COMMERCIAL

6. a. Orchestra Tuning Up - Elvis Enters - Applause
   Walks to gigantic symphony orchestra setting. He
   sx bx bows to conductor, to orchestra.

   b. Eight Minute Symphonic Bit - all his old hits, mixing modern and symphonic sounds, using giant chorus and full orchestra with small group sounds.

   Songs to choose from: "HOUND DOG," "BLUE SUEDE SHOES", "HEARTBREAK HOTEL", "ALL SHOOK UP", "DON'T BE XX CRUEL", "TEDDY BEAR", "WHERE MY RING", "JAILHOUSE ROCK".

7. SECOND COMMERCIAL

8. a. Elvis in quiet talk bit. Shows pictures of his various haircuts, suits, etc. He shows some of his more px peculiar momentos.

   b. Elvis sings sentimental country song.
   Sings: x "COTTON CANDYLAND", "HOW WOULD YOU BE"

   xx c. Finishes big new thing musically (with modern musicians)

9. THIRD COMMERCIAL

10. Gospel Segment

11. FOURTH COMMERCIAL

12. The XXX "MEAN CHUNK"

    Use "GUITAR MAN" as the theme for segment

    Have him continually walking through tape cuts.

(MORE)

"JUST ELVIS" - RUNDOWN PAGE 2.

12. The "MEAN CHUNK" - (Cont'd)

Songs to fit in: "LET YOURSELF GO", "TROUBLE", "LIL' SISTER", "LONG LONELY ROAD", "BIG BOSS MAN", "WHEELS ON MY FEET", "SANTA'S BACK IN TOWN"

13. FIFTH COMMERCIAL

14. a. Christmas Song

b. Elvis Talks

15. Show Closing (not necessarily in this order)

a. Commercial Billboard

b. Crawl

c. NBC Film

Songs listed above: "Long Lonely Road," "Wheels on My Feet," and "Santa's Back In Town" are actually titled "Long Lonely Highway," "Wheels on My Heels," and "Santa Claus Is Back In Town."

According to a June 13th William Morris Agency memo from agent Howard West to David Freedman at NBC, Binder-Howe would be responsible for the writers, choral director, choreographers, and musical conductor/arranger and Teram would be responsible for "The rest of the elements." The contract required a $32,000 one-time payment to Steve Binder for producing and directing that included the first two re-runs of the special. There is no mention of Bones or any salary for his services as the show's music producer (though Bones and I were 50-50 partners on everything we did).

Bones and I tried very hard to protect our interests and control the profits of our creative work. Bones was producing records for "The Fifth Dimension" and "The Association" which earned him royalties, so we thought, since we were producing the sound track to "Elvis," we didn't see why the same rules shouldn't apply. I phoned our agent, Fred Apollo, at the William Morris Agency and explained our position to him. He said he would relay the message to Colonel Parker and at the same time reminded me that Elvis and the Colonel were also William Morris clients but carried a lot more clout at the Agency than Binder-Howe did.

No sooner had I hung up the phone when Fred Apollo phoned me right back and said I had opened up a hornet's nest and the Colonel wanted both of us fired immediately. I maintained that our demand was 100% justifiable. The Colonel was furious and phoned me personally to tell me in no uncertain terms that, "Nobody produces Elvis Presley records but Elvis himself!" and hung up. It was a well-known fact, but not publicized in the business, that if you wanted Elvis to record one of your songs, you had to give over your publishing rights to his company. Bones and I stuck to our guns and didn't back off. Not long after, Fred phoned to say it was all taken care of and we could start back to work.

The solution they all came up with was that nothing in our contract would mention anything about a sound track or records. The Colonel phoned me back and personally gave me his word of honor that there would definitely be no RCA song or soundtrack album released from the television special so we had nothing to worry about. Fred phoned me to back up the Colonel's conversation. I was very naïve and took the Colonel and the William Morris Agency at their word.

Here's the kicker, before the special had even started production, the Colonel made a deal with NBC to turn over the audiotapes from the special to RCA without charge. A deal that would have amounted to millions of dollars in music rights. Elvis got a free album out of the budget of the television special.

And after the special was delivered to NBC, the Colonel mailed to my home a $1,500 check along with an agreement for me to sign waiving all my legal rights to the soundtrack and congratulating me on the release of the album. Instead of signing the agreement, I sent the unsigned check back to the Colonel with a short note telling him where he could put it. To this day, Bones or I have never received one penny from the soundtrack earnings.

I made the decision to start preparing "ELVIS" at our offices on the Sunset Strip instead of driving all the way to NBC in Burbank. Once it was decided what specific songs to use, new arrangements for the songs had to be written in order for Elvis to start rehearsals. I phoned Billy Strange, who I had hired at Elvis's request, to be our music conductor and arranger. Billy informed me that he was busy producing an album for Nancy Sinatra to capitalize on her hit record, "These Boots Are Made For Walking," but assured me that it would be no problem handling both jobs, and I took him at his word. I told him that I had scheduled rehearsals with Elvis, and I would need him to deliver at least the piano arrangements as soon as possible. Every day that followed included a phone call to Billy asking him, "Where are the arrangements, Billy?"

Every day I would get the same answer "They'll be there soon." Finally knowing the day was rapidly approaching when Elvis was to start rehearsing, I phoned Billy and demanded that he deliver a few of the arrangements so that we could start work by the day after tomorrow at 10am sharp or he would be fired. He told me that if it came to one of us being fired, he had the direct line to Elvis and I would be the one to go, and hung up. I immediately phoned Bob Finkel and told him what was going on and he responded with the words "fire him!" I did just that.

When the Colonel found out what I had done he was furious. He told me that he doubted if Elvis would even come to work, so I phoned Elvis and explained the situation to him. His reaction was that it was no big deal. Now I was in a dilemma. Elvis was to rehearse in a few days and I had no music arrangements and no musical director for him to rehearse with.

Enter Billy Goldenberg, who I really wanted to hire in the first place after our collaboration on "Hullabaloo", "Hallelujah, Leslie!" and "Petula." Billy Goldenberg was a key member of our creative family. What I didn't count on was Billy turning me down! When I phoned him at his apartment in New York, Billy explained that he couldn't see himself conducting "Hound Dog" or "Blue Suede Shoes" and that I should get someone else. Billy told me that he grew up in New York and worked on Broadway, not Memphis and even though he'd like to help me out he would have to say no. I told him I was no longer asking him, but on my knees begging him. I guess he heard the desperation in my voice because the next thing I knew Billy was in my office, sitting at our upright piano with Elvis walking through the door.

Billy and Elvis hit it off immediately. Here was this young Jewish kid from New York, a classically trained Broadway composer/conductor/arranger, with the King of Rock 'n' Roll, a southern kid from Tupelo, Mississippi, about to get together in what turned out to be the greatest music collaboration in Elvis' entire career. Billy told me that Elvis loved to play classical music on the piano when nobody was around. His favorite piece was Beethoven's "Moonlight Sonata." Billy said that if some of his guys heard him playing he would stop for fear they would see it as a sign of weakness.

Every day the entourage would drive into our garage in Elvis' Lincoln Continental car with Tennessee license plates. In would walk Elvis, followed by Joe Esposito, Lamar Fike, Alan Fortas, Charlie Hodge, and Lance LeGault (his film stand-in). Arriving by himself, Colonel Parker would sometimes sit in our reception area while Elvis went to work with Billy Goldenberg, Earl Brown, and myself.

Soon after rehearsals at our offices got underway, I saw Elvis looking out at Sunset Blvd. through the window and I asked him what he thought might happen if he walked out there by himself. He turned to me and smiled and asked me what I thought would happen. I thought for a minute and told him that I really didn't think that anything would happen. And we went back to rehearsing.

A few days later, Elvis walked into the office and said to me, "Let's go!" I asked him where to? He said let's go down to the sidewalk on Sunset Blvd. so we can find out. Now it all made sense to me. I'm sure Elvis thought he couldn't go out in public because the Colonel had probably told him he would be mobbed and possibly all his clothes would be torn off with fans trying to get a piece of him. Overhearing our conversation the entourage started heading for the front door like a pack of dogs, but Elvis told them to stay put and watch from the window.

Our building had a unique glass enclosed elevator that looked out onto the street while going up or down. Directly across the street from our office building was a club called the "Classic Cat," and though I never went inside, I assumed it was a highbrow topless club. There were hardly any pedestrians on the street, but the traffic was building on the Strip with commuters and delivery trucks hurrying to their destinations. It was a little awkward for both of us because we feigned some conversation about nothing particularly important. We were both waiting for something to happen. Cars were driving by, not even bothering to look at us. No horns were honking and no California Girls were rolling down their windows to get a look at Elvis or scream out his name. A couple of seedy looking hippies almost bumped into us as they were heavily engaged in their own conversation.

After a long few minutes, I could tell Elvis was getting uncomfortable and restless. Absolutely nothing unusual was happening and I sensed the window upstairs was filled with his guys making wisecracks about us. A few more minutes passed before Elvis decided to take charge of the situation. He started waving at the passengers in the cars passing by. Still nothing happened. Elvis had enough and wanted go inside.

I am still convinced that had anyone known in advance that it was really Elvis Presley standing outside on the street, the traffic would have come to a standstill and girls would have been jumping out of the cars and pouring out of surrounding office buildings. None of this happened because Hollywood is filled with guys who want to look like Elvis, and everybody passing by thought it was just another wanna-be. When we went back upstairs, I sensed a subtly different attitude in my relationship with Elvis. From that point forward until the end of the shoot, he kept asking my opinion about everything.

Elvis had learned to trust me.

6/26/68

2ND REVISED RUNDOWN "ELVIS" STARRING ELVIS PRESLEY TAPE: 6/27-29/68 AIR: 12/3/68

1. Disclaimer (1)
2. Peacock (2)
3. "GUITAR MAN" Opening (3)
   Elvis, 89 Boys
4. Opening Commercial (8)
   Billboard
5. FIRST COMMERCIAL (9)
6. Arena Segment
   "LITTLE LESS CONVERSATION" (10)
7. Arena Talk (14)
   Elvis
8. Arena
   Elvis
   a. "HEARTBREAK HOTEL" (15)
   b. "HOUND DOG" (17)
   c. "ALL SHOOK UP" (19)
   d. "FALLING IN LOVE WITH YOU" (22)
   e. "JAILHOUSE ROCK" (24)
   f. "DON'T BE CRUEL" (27)
   g. "BLUE SUEDE SHOES" (29)
   h. "LOVE ME TENDER" (33)
9. SECOND COMMERCIAL (38)
10. Informal Segment
    a. Talk & Songs (39)
    b. "MEMORIES" (46)
11. THIRD COMMERCIAL (48)
12. Gospel Medley (49)
    Elvis, Blossoms, Dancers

REVISED RUNDOWN - "ELVIS" 2.

13. FOURTH COMMERCIAL (61)
14. "GUITAR MAN" Segment
    a. Road One (62)
       Elvis
    b. Alley Scene (63)
       Elvis, Men
    c. "LET YOURSELF GO" (65)
       Elvis, Girls
    d. Road Two (70)
       Elvis
    e. Amusement Pier (72)
       Elvis, Dancers, Bits
    f. Road Three (79)
       Elvis
    g. Club (81)
       Elvis, Dancers, Bits
15. FIFTH COMMERCIAL (86)
16. "IF I CAN DREAM" (87)
    Elvis
17. Goodnights (90)
    Elvis
18. Commercial Billboard (91)
19. Closing Credits (92)
    Elvis
20. NBC Production Tag (92)

"What clinched it for us is when Steve said, "I have this idea of a wonderful dance sequence with all karate moves. Elvis lit up like a Christmas tree. He said let me talk with the Colonel about this. Next thing I know were are doing the Elvis Presley special."

— BONES HOWE, Music Production

Chapter 2

Western Recorders

Some of the most exciting hours spent with Elvis were at the pre-recording sessions from June 20 to the 23rd at Western Recorders Studios, located at 6000 Sunset Boulevard in Hollywood.

Western Recorders had a long history of being the place to record music because of their state of the art facilities and recording expertise. I can personally remember going to a session there a few years earlier to watch Frank Sinatra record one of his great albums. Bones was using Western to record many of his hit records with The Fifth Dimension and The Association. It wasn't easy convincing NBC to record at Western. Earlier on, when we announced to NBC that we were hiring freelance musicians and going to an outside facility to record they typically resisted. Word came down that it would cost too much money and why couldn't we use the same musicians that Bob Hope used on his specials and record at NBC? Bones and I knew that wouldn't work for Elvis so we set out to get the best the rock 'n' roll musicians we could find and stood our ground.

When Elvis arrived at the studio and walked into Studio One, he saw a studio with 35 of the greatest west coast musicians ready to play on the soundtrack of his special, including some of the best studio rhythm men in the entire world: Hal Blaine and Johnny Cyr on drums and percussion, Don Randi on piano and organ, Chuck Berghoffer on bass, and Mike Deasy, Al Casey, Tommy Tedesco and Larry Knechtal on guitars. Elvis was panicked. He called me out onto Sunset Blvd. and made me promise that if he didn't like the sound of the orchestra, I would send them all home except for the rhythm section. The first thought that occurred to me was that he might be unsure of Billy Goldenberg's rock 'n' roll arrangements since he had really never heard even one Billy Goldenberg arrangement, but was going on my word that he would be great. To my surprise, he confessed to me that he never sang with anything but a rhythm section that consisted of no more than a guitar, bass and drums. He told me that he didn't even know if he would know how to sing with such a large orchestra. I gave him my word that I would send all of the musicians home and only keep the rhythm section, but ONLY on the condition that he give it a try.

We walked back into the room of waiting musicians and Elvis stepped up along side of Billy Goldenberg standing on his conductor's two-foot riser above the orchestra. They nodded at one another and Billy gave the downbeat to the orchestra on "Guitar Man." Need I say more? The recording sessions were a blast. Tommy Morgan was sensational playing the harmonica and all the musicians were having the time of their lives. On a coffee break, I remember accidentally hearing Mike Deasy and Tommy Tedesco fooling around and creating a scratching sound on their guitars. I loved what I heard. I went to Bones and asked that after the short break we record about two minutes of them scratching away and I used the sound right after the Guitar Man as an underscore to the main opening and end titles. I still love the sound every time I hear it.

Western Recorders Left to RIght: Bones Howe, Steve Binder, and legendary drummer Hal Blaine.

Bones Howe at the control panel and Steve Binder consulting with script supervisor Pat Rickey.

Even though I was going to have Elvis sing live to the track of "If I Can Dream", the story of that memorable day still stays with me. After the last note of the orchestra was played and the musicians packed up their instruments and headed out the door, Elvis came to me and asked if he could put his vocal on the track to practice with since he really wasn't that familiar with the lyrics. I informed Bones and the recording engineer what was about to happen and we locked the door to the studio and set-up for Elvis to record once again. The only people left in the studio were Elvis, Bones, and Pat Rickey, my script supervisor, the recording engineer, his utility man and myself. It was getting late in the evening and we had been working steadily since very early that morning. The boom microphone was set up in the middle of the stage and Elvis put his headset on so he could listen to the track while he sang. His voice boomed: "I'm ready Bones, you can roll the tape," and Bones did. Elvis sang the lyrics and we all thought we were going home knowing his vocal was never going to be used other than for Elvis to listen to.

Just as I was about to say goodnight to Elvis on the intercom, Elvis's voice boomed out again. "I'd like to try it one more time if you don't mind but this time with a hand mike." I don't think anyone else but Elvis ever made such a request singing a vocal in a recording studio. The normal set-up included an overhead boom or stand microphone, a music stand to place the lead sheet with the lyrics to the song and the vocalist isolated in a soundproof booth. This would protect the vocal from leaking into other open microphones on the stage. Bones gave the word to his utility engineer, and we were about to begin.

At the last minute I asked that all the lights be turned out in the large and now empty studio. The only lights left on were the panel lights on Bone's' mixing board and the lights on the tape meters and tape machines. It was an eerie feeling, but it certainly set a mood. Looking out from the control booth glass into the studio, you could barely see the outline of Elvis standing in front of all of the empty chairs and music stands. Bones started the tape playback and as Elvis started to sing, something totally unexpected happened. After the first verse of the song, Elvis dropped to the floor clutching his microphone and assumed a fetal position forgetting where he was or who was watching him. What surprised me at the time the most was that he had already memorized the words. It was all that basic instinct coming out through his entire being and forming the words to the song as they escaped his throat. It was animal, raw and powerful.

As great a performance as it was to an audience of five, I still made the decision to have him sing live to the track when we taped "If I Can Dream" at NBC. I admit that the television taping came nowhere close to his performance at the recording studio, but I still stand by my decision to have him sing live rather than have him lip sync on television.

RECEIVED FROM CHARLIE THE FOLLOWING DUBS:

"SAVED" - LEIBER & STOLLER (W/lead sheet)

("CAN YOU FIND IT IN YOUR HEART - TEPPER & BENNETT (W/Lead sheet)
xx

:LET'S FORGET ABOUT THE STARS" - A.B. Owens (w/Lead sheet)

K

RECEIVED FROM CHARLIE THE FOLLOWING 45:

"NOT ME" ("Truckstop Romance") - w/lead sheet for "Not Me" (Tepper - Bennett)

Pat

PAT RICKEY
6/4/68

To Pat the Great
Who set around
every thing in fact.
Tee Dee

June 17, 1968

Colonel Tom Parker
Elvis Exploitations
MGM Studios
10202 West Washington Blvd.
Culver City, California 90230

Dear Colonel Parker:

Would you request from MGM a release of the master tape of "A Little Less Conversation." We would like their permission to use this master tape for the Elvis Presley Special, to be aired December 3, 1968. We also would like a composite minus Elvis' voice so that he can sing live to the track on the show.

Sincerely,

Steve

STEVE BINDER
Producer

SB:lm

c.c: Mr. Bob Finkel

Steve Binder and Elvis shown here at the first night of recording at Western Recorders.

Chapter 3

Press Conference

What became very clear to Bones and I was that Elvis had a fantastic sense of humor that for the most part was never revealed to the public and now here was a chance for the media to see it. At 6:15PM on Tuesday, June 25th, the Colonel scheduled a press conference at NBC to promote the special. Yellow neck scarves with small scarf holders were handed out to all of us from the Colonel as gifts from Elvis for us to wear when we entered the make shift pressroom. Truthfully I hated wearing scarves. They always made me feel uncomfortable and especially knowing that we were wearing some kind of Elvis 'uniform.' As we walked into the room, Elvis said, "Come on Steve, these are always fun."

The Colonel placed himself in back of the room and stood behind the press corps seated on metal folding chairs. We were seated at a large table in front of the packed room of anxious reporters. Even where we were seated was choreographed by the Colonel. At the end of the long table facing the press was Lamar Fike and Bones Howe. I was seated next to Bones with Elvis next to me on my left. Elvis was wearing a tailored silk shirt and smoking his favorite stogie cigar. On the other side of Elvis, was Bob Finkel in an all white suit and also smoking a stogie that Elvis handed him just as we entered the room. Joe Esposito, Charlie Hodge and Alan Fortas stood behind us.

When we entered the room and took our places at the table, I noticed a stack of Elvis brochures for the press to take with them when the conference ended. The front of the table was covered with black velour material so we could only be seen from our chests up. Every time a question was directed to Elvis that he thought was stupid and before he answered the question, he would bang his leg against mine under the table signaling me that he was about to give a funny or stupid answer back. Typical questions asked in the press conference were: Reporter: ""Elvis, why are you doing this show?" Elvis: "We figured it was about time. Besides, I thought I'd better do it before I got too old." Colonel Parker (from in back of the room) "We also got a very good deal." Reporter: "Has your audience changed much?" Elvis: "Well, they don't move as fast as they used to". When it seemed that we were just starting to enjoy the exchanges with Elvis and the press, the conference ended abruptly. From the back of the room, the Colonel, like the puppet master that he was, told everyone that the press conference was over, and with that we all got up and left the room.

Left to right: Bones Howe, Steve Binder, Elvis, Bob Finkle, and Joe Esposito.

"We got our money's worth out of Elvis. The special was a big event and I thought the special was terrific."

—TOM SARNOFF, NBC Vice President, Production and Business Affairs

"There was a lot of inventiveness and creativity about his work and that's why I chose Steve."

— BOB FINKEL, Executive Producer

Warm-Up Rehearsal

Chapter 4

The Improv

The informal section for me was what we called the money shot in the show. Elvis had no concept that there were cameras shooting him. He was so into the moment, Elvis was having a ball and the public had never seen this side of him before. Elvis was having the time of his life and once he realized the studio audience loved him, he simply could not give them enough.

Here is the story of how it all came about. Elvis was so impressed with the king size star dressing rooms adjoining Stage 4 at NBC that he made the decision to move in and live there while we were taping the special. On entering its enormous living room with its baby grand piano, you could walk through a door to a separate dressing room, walk-in shower and bathroom. Elvis requested that we put an upright piano in the small room in back.

It was in that living room that after every day of shooting on stage, Elvis and his entourage would hang out and unwind by singing and telling stories until all hours of the night. These moments became my inspiration for the improvisation sessions. In contrast to the sweet, innocent hero image that we were taping on stage, here was this raw, sexual and playful Elvis backstage in his converted dressing room/ bedroom. I sensed the King was coming back to regain his throne.

Once production was underway, the sessions in the dressing room lasted three or four hours after the days work on the stage. There were Dutch cigars and Pepsi's everywhere. The sessions were spirited and directionless. The guys would sing and tell stories about each other and laugh their heads off. They started with Elvis, Charlie, Alan, Lance, Joe and Lamar and later, joined by Scotty Moore and D.J. Fontana when the decision was made to put it on tape.

Every night, Elvis would make his way to his dressing room / living quarters. There was no sign of fatigue and I would listen to him unwind with his guitar and a few 'invited' friends. They'd be having the time of their lives in a plain ol' jam session. For me, it was like looking inside a keyhole and seeing something that nobody else in the whole world was supposed to be seeing.

The sessions lasted for 4 or 5 hours or until Elvis wanted to go to bed. There was a lot of laughter, storytelling and above all music. Songs from the past like: "Are You Lonesome Tonight," "Love Me" and "When My Blue Moon Turns to Gold Again." There were raw and raunchy songs like: "That's All Right," "Lawdy Miss Clawdy" and "Blue Christmas." The guys joked about Finkel and myself and told stories about seeing nude women in front of open windows and old times on the road. One story was about the time Elvis was in Florida and the police threatened to arrest him if he moved his lower body so for the entire concert he just wiggled his little finger.

Above all, I was watching an Elvis that I knew his fans hadn't seen since 1954 when Sam Phillips, owner of Sun Records, recorded and released his first record "That's All Right," and Elvis performed his first live concert that same year at the Louisiana Hayride in Shreveport, with guitarist Scotty Moore and bassist Bill Black.

It was raw and powerful and it was all coming back to him. I knew that I had to tape this because no matter how clever we were in planning a rehearsed and scripted show, what I was seeing with no director, no writers, no sets or costumes involved, was the real Elvis. I asked the Colonel if I could bring my camera into the dressing room and record what was going on. He said in no uncertain terms no chance in hell. Leaving me no alternative, I then snuck in my little hidden Sony mini tape audio recorder, a pencil and pad and just started taking notes. I just had to change the Colonel's mind.

Before I even had a chance to convince him, the Colonel, out of the blue a few days later, told me that if I wanted to recreate what was happening in the dressing room, he'd let me do it on stage. But he added that I'd be wasting my time. "Remember," he said, "This is only a one-hour Christmas special and there's no time to put this crap in." Getting to at the very least recreate the dressing room jam sessions was definitely better than nothing at all and I'd try to figure out how to use this material later.

When I explained to Elvis what my plan was, he insisted that he'd need Scotty and D.J. Fontana, his drummer, to do it with him. "There's not a guitar player in Hollywood that can play like Scotty," he said, and tried to demonstrate to me on his guitar the 'lick' that Scotty could play that he couldn't, and felt that nobody else could either. We immediately organized their trip to L.A., and set the wheels in motion with the staff to prepare a special taping day for the improvisational sessions.

I decided to do two shows in one day with two completely different audiences. In a meeting with Bill Belew and Gene McAvoy, we decided to use elements of the set that was already built and Bill thought that the black leather suit that he designed for the orchestra medley early on in the show would be appropriate.

I insisted that there would be no electric amplifiers used in this segment so there wouldn't be any similarity or duplication between the orchestra segment and the improvisational segments. I told Gene McAvoy not to set up D.J.'s drum kit. He would have to play his drums sticks on top of Elvis' guitar case. We were all, by normal standards 'crazy'. I was flying by the seat of my pants and in 1968 an entire acoustic session had never been done before on television. Rock musicians were used to turning their amplifiers up as loud as they could possibly go before blowing out the speakers. But, this was "Elvis" and we were willing to take chances, especially since we had gotten this far and hadn't been fired yet!

When Allan and Chris received word that the improvisational segment was 'on,' they immediately raced to their typewriters and banged out a script for Elvis to read. Of course, I had absolutely no intention of using it because it would defeat the whole purpose of having Elvis do an improvisational segment that was off-the-cuff, honest and a chance to look through that magic keyhole and see the REAL Elvis. This was the opportunity of a lifetime. But if you're curious to see what they wrote, here it is:

INFORMAL TALK AND SONGS:

Have you ever thought what it's like to be an Elvis Presley? In the beginning when we were singing all those country songs back in Memphis I never thought about it much. Then one day we took the country and western sound and mixed it with a little colored soul, and all hell broke loose. People started to recognize me in the street......I've got to admit, I really got a kick out of that. Guys would just walk up to me and say, "Are you really Elvis Presley? And I'd say, "Yeah." I'd stick my hand out to shake hands with 'em...they'd hit me right in the mouth and take off.... That's when I knew I'd made it....Since then I've been put in the hospital thirty-seven times just for being Elvis Presley!!! I really got into trouble doing my "thing" in those days. In Los Angeles I was told I had to stand still while performing...I couldn't touch my body with my hands in

Philadelphia...and on network television, I couldn't be shot from the waist down. So this show is a real breakthrough for me. As you can see, I can now be shot from the waist down... (TAKE A SHOT) Pretty exciting, huh? I can touch my body with my hands (HE DOES) And I don't have to stand still while performing. (SINGS) "You Ain't Nothing But A Hound Dog" (HURTS HIMSELF - HOLDS SIDE) Well, that ain't as easy as it used to be I'll tell you! But that's all in the past.... Being Elvis Presley today is a whole different bag. I've got the sideburns back because they're in again. But the three-inch pompadour is gone; along with the upper left lip scowl...Remember that? I did the entire production of "Jailhouse Rock" on that look alone, baby! I did a lot of moves...and I've done a lot of songs in those movies. And here's a few toe-tappers that'll really knock your hat in the creek. You remember this one....

MUSIC: "COTTON CANDY LAND" (ELVIS ONLY)

SANDMAN'S COMIN'

YES HE'S COMING

TO SPRINKLE YOU WITH SAND

HE'LL SAY ONE, TWO, THREE

AND YOU WILL BE

IN COTTON CANDY LAND

(SPEAKS)

And then there was...

MUSIC: "HOW WOULD YOU LIKE TO BE" (ELVIS ONLY)

HOW WOULD YOU LIKE TO BE

A LITTLE CIRCUS CLOWN

AND YOU COULD WEAR A SMILE

INSTEAD OF THAT FROWN

HOW WOULD YOU LIKE TO BE

A LITTLE KANGAROO

A-HOPPIN' UP AND DOWN

AND I COULD HOP WITH YOU

COME ON AND SMILE A LITTLE

SMILE A LITTLE

HOP A LITTLE, HOP A LITTLE

SMILE A LITTLE

HOP A LITTLE BIT WITH ME

SMILE A LITTLE, SMILE A LITTLE

HOP A LITTLE HOP A LITTLE

SMILE A LITTLE

HOP A LITTLE BIT WITH ME

OH HO AH HA

TRA LA LA LA LA LA LA

AH HA

TRA LA LA LA LA LA LA

(SPEAKS)

This one everybody seemed to like...and so did I for a change!!

MUSIC: "WOODEN HEART" (ELVIS ONLY)

CAN'T YOU SEE

I LOVE YOU

PLEASE DON'T BREAK

MY HEART IN TWO

THAT'S NOT HARD TO DO

CAUSE I DON'T

HAVE A WOODEN HEART

AND IF YOU SAY GOODBYE

THEN I KNOW

THAT I WOULD CRY

MAYBE I WOULD DIE

CAUSE I DON'T

HAVE A WOODEN HEART

THERE'S NO STRINGS UPON

THIS LOVE OF MINE

IT WAS ALWAYS YOU

FROM THE START

TREAT ME NICE

TREAT ME GOOD

TREAT ME LIKE YOU REALLY SHOULD

CAUSE I'M NOT MADE OF WOOD

AND I DON'T HAVE

A WOODEN HEART

(GERMAN LYRICS TO COME)

THERE'S NO STRINGS UPON

THIS LOVE OF MINE

IT WAS ALWAYS YOU

FROM THE START

(GERMAN LYRICS TO COME)

CAUSE I DON'T

HAVE A WOODEN HEART

(SPEAKS)

Making movies is an experience that's hard to put into words...You know my movies. I'm usually the "goodie goodie" singing mechanic who always gets the girl...A lot of people ask me what I think of today's music. I'll never forget a couple of years ago, the Beatles came out to my house, and the first one I met was Ringo Starr. I said to him, "Are you really Ringo Starr?" He said, "Yeah, baby." I hit him right in the mouth! And Ringo said, "Now I know I really made it!" (LAUGH) I really like Beatle music, and a lot of the other music that's happening today....I like the way they sound, and I like what they're saying....

(INTO: "MEMORIES")

I went to the Colonel and asked if he needed any audience tickets to the improvisational sessions. He looked at me funny as if he didn't think I was going to actually tape the improv even after he gave me the okay. He told me that if I wanted to see the real Elvis fans and not "Your Hollywood phonies," I would have to give him all the tickets and he'd make sure the audience would be filled with Memphis teenagers with blue eyes and bouffant hairdos. He said, "Not one ticket could be given to an executive, sponsor or employee of my staff and crew."

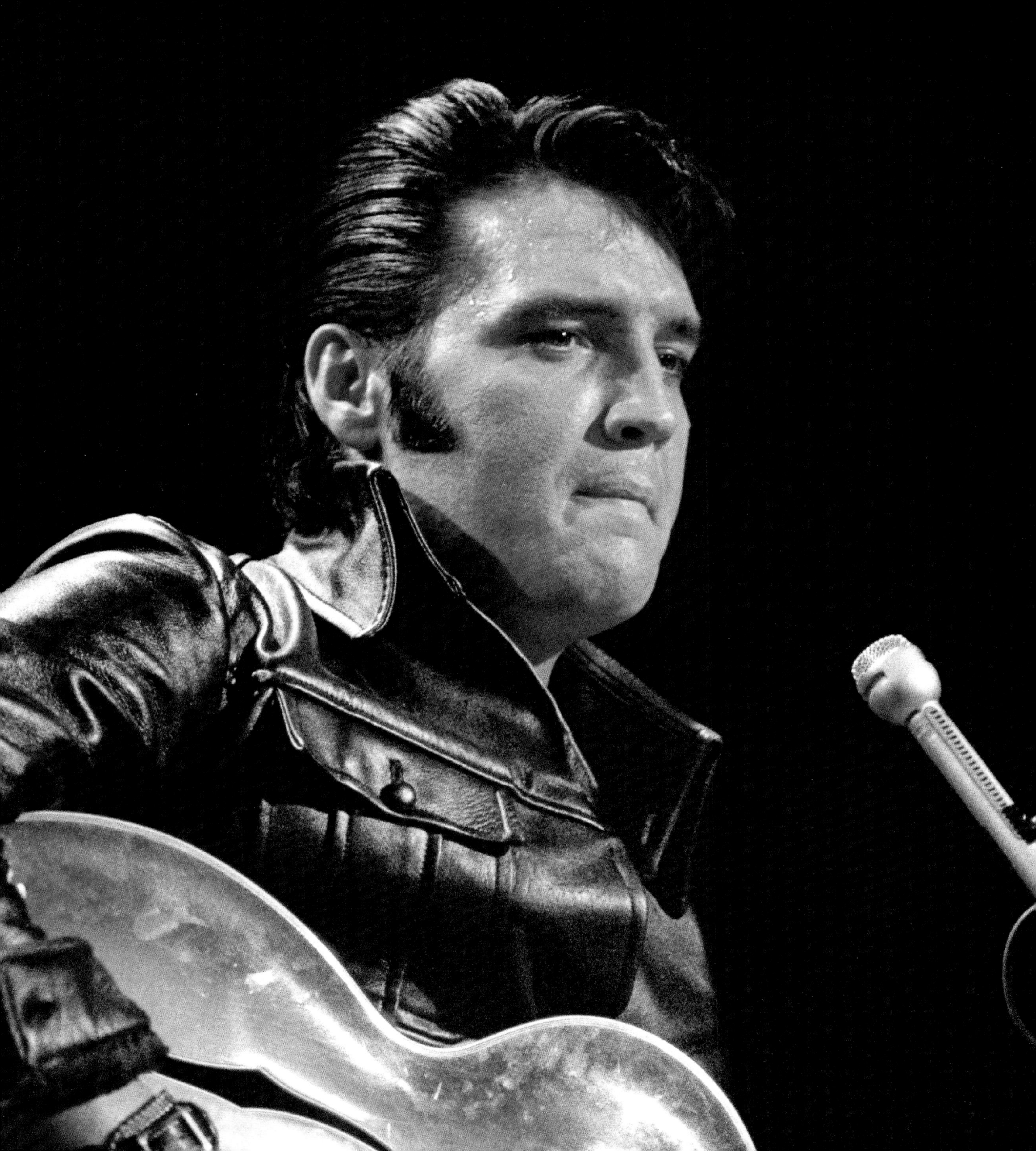

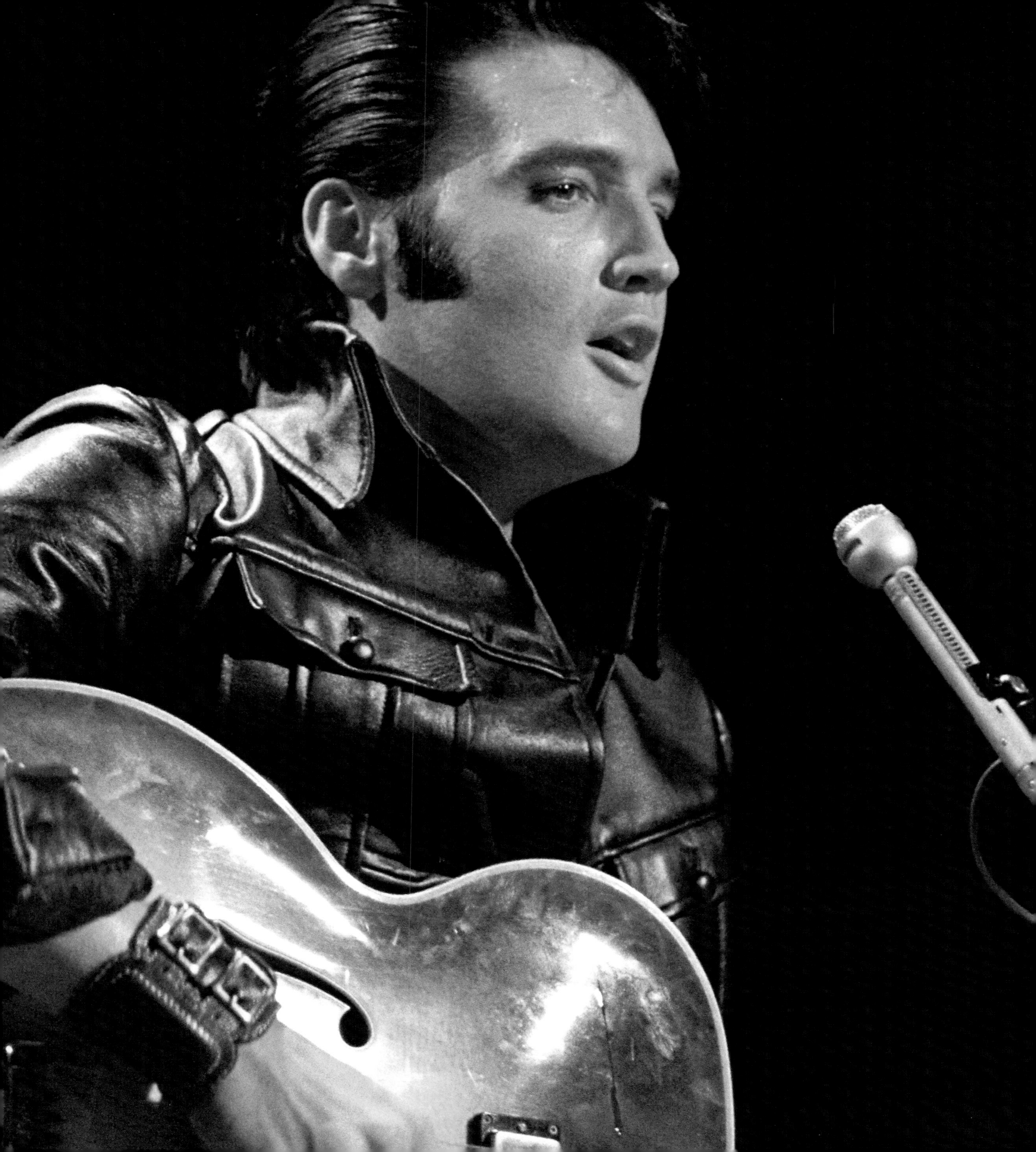

I didn't have the authority to tell the executives or the sponsor's representatives that they couldn't come to the taping, so I immediately went to Finkel and explained the situation to him. Bob came through again. He instructed me to give all the tickets to the Colonel and he would handle NBC and the sponsors.

It came as a shock to the Colonel when I handed him all the tickets. I visualized this giant airplane flying out of Memphis with hundreds of pure and unadulterated Elvis Presley fanatics chomping at the bit to see their idol up close. Wouldn't you think the same?

The night before the actual taping I called a meeting with the guest relations department to warn them about crowd control the next morning. We agreed on adding additional NBC ushers and even spoke of contacting the Burbank police department if the crowd got out of control. It seemed that I had covered all the bases except one. Driving off the lot that evening the guard on duty at the gate having no clue who I was, asked me if I needed any tickets for tomorrow's "ELVIS" show. At first I took it as a joke until I saw a huge stack of our tickets on the desk inside the shack. I couldn't believe my eyes. But even then I didn't panic. I thought the Colonel wouldn't need the tickets when his airplane arrived. He'd probably be bussing them in.

I could barely sleep that night in anticipation for what was about to happen. I headed to Burbank exceptionally early in the morning to see with my own eyes what was happening outside the studio. We were scheduled to start taping in the late afternoon. When I arrived at the studio, a few people were starting to collect outside on Alameda Street so I still wasn't panicking. As soon as I walked in the door, I was told that the people I saw were probably the extra pages hired to handle the overflow audiences.

It was then I realized the Colonel had duped me. There was to be no airplane filled with screaming teenagers from Tennessee to see Elvis in person. The Colonel had merely given all the tickets to the NBC gate guards or more likely thrown them away. I panicked. Bones said he'd phone a few radio disc jockeys in Los Angeles and have them ask their audience to come to the NBC Burbank Studios to see Elvis in person. We sent our people to a drive-in restaurant close to NBC named "Bob's Big Boy" which specialized in hamburgers and malted milkshakes. They literally walked up to cars with people eating their lunches asking them if they wanted to see Elvis in person. When it came time to tape, we had gathered a group made up of last minute invitees and any secretary or relative that could come to Stage 4.

Just before we were about to tape, Elvis asked to see me. I found him in the make-up room. When I entered he asked the woman applying his make-up to leave. Elvis said that it was not that he wasn't willing to, but he didn't know what to say or sing when he got out there. It had all gone away. I got out a piece of paper and in the next few minutes scribbled down from memory what stories he told and what songs he sang and in no time filled up a page and handed it to him. I shoved the paper into his hand, looked him straight in the eye and said calmly, "Elvis do this for me! If you get out there and really can't think of anything to say or sing, then say hello to the audience and come on back." I headed for the control room to give the command to roll tape.

Scotty, D.J., Charlie, and Alan and were already on the small stage seated on blue leather and metal chairs. Bassist Chuck Berghoffer was placed off camera and Lance LeGault, with tambourine in hand was below the stage next to where Elvis would be sitting prepared to hand up any of Elvis's many guitars. The Colonel was placing the 'prettiest girls' on the steps and stage close to where Elvis would be sitting while Robert W. Morgan, a local DJ from KHJ radio was warming up the audience. The stage was fifteen feet by fifteen feet and painted red, white and black. The spillover audience was seated in bleachers surrounding the stage. "Get them close to Elvis" the Colonel barked. "Who here really loves Elvis?" The carnival was about to begin.

The lights dimmed and we heard the roar of the crowd starting to swell. I had my fingers crossed that it would somehow how work out well. "Please God" I said to myself, and then as if my prayer was answered, there he was. Elvis Presley, finding his way back home. He worked his way through the crowd, climbing the steps to his awaiting chair and just stood there for what seemed like eternity taking in the crowd before he picked up his guitar. I was fascinated just watching him looking at the audience. He smiled, sat down, and started talking. He thanked the audience for coming and joked about not knowing what he was supposed to do. He even pretended to fall asleep. But the minute he picked up his guitar and started to sing "That's All Right," I knew I could finally relax. His lifeblood oozed out of every pore in his body. On that chair he never sat still. He squirmed on it like the seat was made of glass. It was like the evening jam sessions in the dressing room, only now Elvis was the sweaty, sexy, fertility God, dressed in black leather that matched the color of his boots and jet black hair. "Ma'h Boy! Ma'h Boy!" he repeated over and over again, knowing he was home. Elvis Presley was back to reclaim his crown as the King of Rock 'n' Roll.

Days earlier, when Elvis was afraid he wouldn't know how to end the improvisation taping in front of a live audience, we devised a signal that when I sensed it was over, I would cue the track to "Memories" as I thought it would be the perfect ending to the session. Elvis would wrap up the end of the song he was singing, walk through the audience of young women seated around him and come downstage to the steps. I gave him no direction once he was there. I felt he would know what to do. When the first taping was completed, we took a break to bring in a fresh audience, find Elvis a guitar strap, and put a rug on the floor of the stage to dampen the sound of their stomping boots.

Unfortunately, because the final edit of the special was 60 minutes, the improv segments were only used as inners and outers, transitions to the production numbers.

But eventually, the out-take reels had a life of their own. The funny story behind it is that I got a phone call from the people who owned the RCA specials in New York and a gentleman named Joe Rascoff who was the business manager of the Elvis Presley estate for awhile. And they said, "We just worked out a deal with RCA and we're going to do another Elvis Presley tribute show. Do you have any ideas?" And I said, "Absolutely." I said "You don't even have to pay a penny for it.

I continued, "In the vault at Bekins is two hours of the most incredible Elvis Presley out-take footage that exists." They didn't know what I was talking about, so I got a letter from Rascoff which authorized me to go to Bekins, and that's when I yanked out the two masters.

I brought them the tapes and after watching them, they called me up and said, "Do you think anybody cares about this stuff?" I mean, it blew my mind. I said, "Just play it in front of an Elvis Presley fan and there's your answer."

They went ahead and sold the tapes to HBO for, I heard, a million dollars for what would become the special "One Night with You." Just for the right to air it. It became one of HBO's highest rated shows to this day on their cable network.

"One Night With You" **IS** Elvis Presley and proved he wasn't just a myth of the Colonel and RCA's PR machine. It even proved to Elvis that he **was** special. I think in the very beginning and the reason that Elvis thought that doing the special in the first place might be a bad idea, was because he had lost confidence in himself and his own abilities to succeedd in front of a live audience. He was actually afraid to fail and expressed these thoughts to me early on. Once he started taping the special, I could visually see him gain his energy, excitement and confidence in himself that had been missing from his life.

And today, every foot of video is now out on DVD, including my director intercom dialogue to the stage between Elvis and myself.

"Steve just told us to go out there and have a good time and we did. We had a ball out there."

— DJ FONTANA

"I didn't realize until later that we actually did the first unplugged session that came down the pipe."

— SCOTTY MOORE

Left to right: Elvis, Charles Hodge, Scotty Moore, Alan Fortas, and DJ Fontana

Left to right: Lance Legault, Elvis, and (back-turned) Charles Hodge

"Seeing the '68 Special on the big screen with a full audience at the Cinerama Dome in May 2008 brought back a lot of good memories. My favorite part of the Special is the sitdown show – the real Elvis I knew comes through in that part of the show, jamming with friends, everyone just knowing what everyone else was doing. I'm so glad the Special has lasted this long and drew an audience from all over the world. Scooch over puppies, the big dog's back in town."

—LANCE LEGAULT

"I don't remember screaming – we were in the moment. I was listening to every word Elvis sang, didn't want to scream. I didn't want to miss a word of his singing."

—JOAN GANSKY - audience member

"Going to the taping was one of the most exciting things I have ever done as an Elvis fan. When he sang "All Shook Up," Elvis looked right at me and I tried not to scream."

—JUDY PALMER - audience member

Chapter 5

Production Numbers

TROUBLE/GUITAR MAN OPENING:

I was walking on the NBC lot one day when Allan Blye came to me with a great idea. He asked if it was possible to hire 100 Elvis look-alikes for the opening number. He explained in detail how he visualized seeing Elvis' face in a close-up and when the camera pulled back it would reveal the 100 Elvis clones playing their guitars behind him. I felt it would be a sensational opening statement, so I went to Bob Finkel who after hearing the idea, promised that he would do his best to make it happen.

As an after thought Bob yelled at me, "How many minutes of airtime will you be using them for?" I yelled back, "Probably no more than two minutes." I turned around just in time to see him scratching the back of his head and walking away. I smiled to myself and said it would probably be a hard sell to the front office. I have always felt in all of my shows that if there's just one memorable moment caught on camera, you never want to repeat it again. People will remember it forever. If you show it twice in the same show it loses its impact. Many have since tried to imitate the "Elvis" opening so it must have been one of those moments.

We got the word that Finkel had received approval from the front office to hire the look-alikes. Now my problem was where to put them. I vividly remembered the Judy Garland show and its set, and especially the signature use of her name "JUDY" spelled out in lights twenty or thirty feet above the floor. I asked Gene McAvoy, our art director, to do the same for "ELVIS." We had already made the decision in our 'think tank' that the entire special would be color coordinated with only black and red scenery with the exception of wardrobe.

100 Elvises sounded like a great idea when I first heard the idea, but when I actually placed even the 89 we actually hired in the set, there wasn't enough room to put them all in individual spaces. When I saw them stacked one in front of another, I should have let a few of them go, but I didn't have the heart to fire anyone. Now in hindsight, I know I had too many Elvises to compose the picture the way it should have been shot.

The first time we tried the shot pulling back from Elvis's close-up to reveal the set behind him, we started applauding in the booth. Elvis, dressed in black with a red bandana around his neck and the camera ever so slowly pulling back to reveal a 30 foot wall of Elvis look-alikes playing their guitars directly behind him, sent chills down my spine.

Following our show opening was a big production number with a cast of 80, using all 35 dancers, with extras, multiple sets, costumes and props. Allan and Chris had woven a medley of songs telling a story about an innocent, small town boy who loves to play his guitar. The young guitar man sets out to explore the world and finds himself traveling and performing on his road to success. The set representing the road was yellow neon tubing against a black velour scenic flat. His journey takes him to a carnival boardwalk, a house of ill repute, a small seedy dance bar, an upscale nightclub and a stadium arena. Now this was conceived in our think-tank to represent an old story about a young brother and sister pursuing their escaped pet bluebird. The children leave home to find their cherished pet. After many scary adventures, they come home to find the bluebird safe at home in its cage. It also paralleled, in some ways, Elvis's real life.

GUITAR MAN

OPENING

MUSIC CUE GUITAR MAN.

(THE CAMERA COMES UP ON A GIGANTIC LOOK OF ONE HUNDRED ELVIS LOOK-A-LIKES STANDING IN HUGE SEE THRU SKYSCRAPER. THAT COVERS THE ENTIRE STUDIO.) (THEY MOVE TO THE "GUITAR MAN" INTRO. IN ELVIS FASHION.) AT THE END OF THE INTRO WE CUT. TO. C.U. OF ELVIS. LOOKING RIGHT INTO CAMERA.) ELVIS SINGS "GUITAR MAN" RIGHT ~~THROUGH~~. (WE USE SET AND ELVIS LOOK-A-LIKES. DURING NUMBER. CUTTING WIDE AND FOR C.U.'S) (ON LAST VERSE WE GO BACK INTO MEDIUM CU AND STAY.) (AT THE TAG OF THE NUMBER WE ~~[illegible] TO REVEAL~~ ~~ELVIS [illegible] ALONE IN THE~~

(~~WE~~ STOP TAPE.)

(WE START TO PULL
OUT REVEALING ~~THAT~~
ELVIS ~~IS~~ NOW ALONE
IN THE ~~GIANT~~ SKYSCRAPER
LOOK, AND WE NOW
~~HAVE~~ THE SINGLE GIANT WORD
"ELVIS" ~~AS A PART~~ OF
THE LOOK.) spelled out in lights

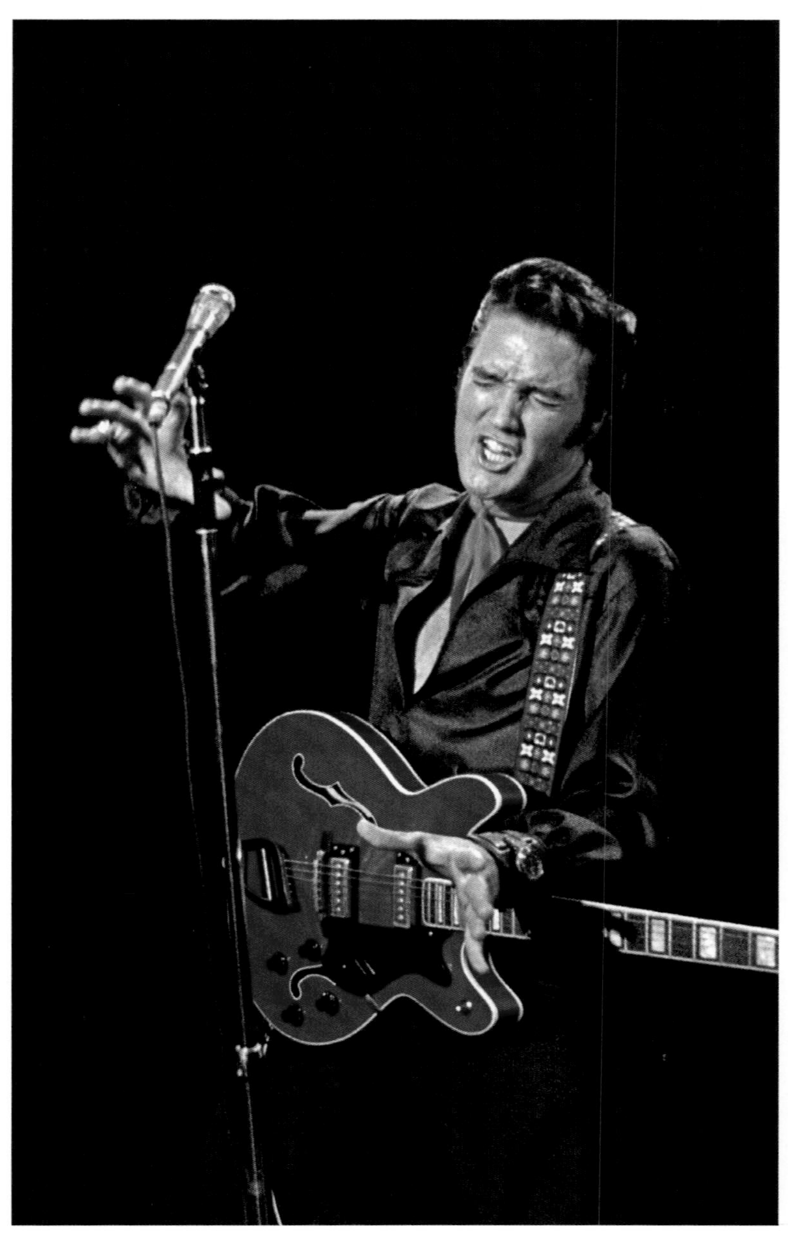

OPENING Commercial BILLBOARDS.

WE USE THE EDITECH TECNIQUE, FREEZE FRAMING THE VIDEOTAPE OF ELVIS MOVING IN TIME WITH THE BILLBOARD INTRODUCTION MUSIC

FIRST COMMERCIAL.

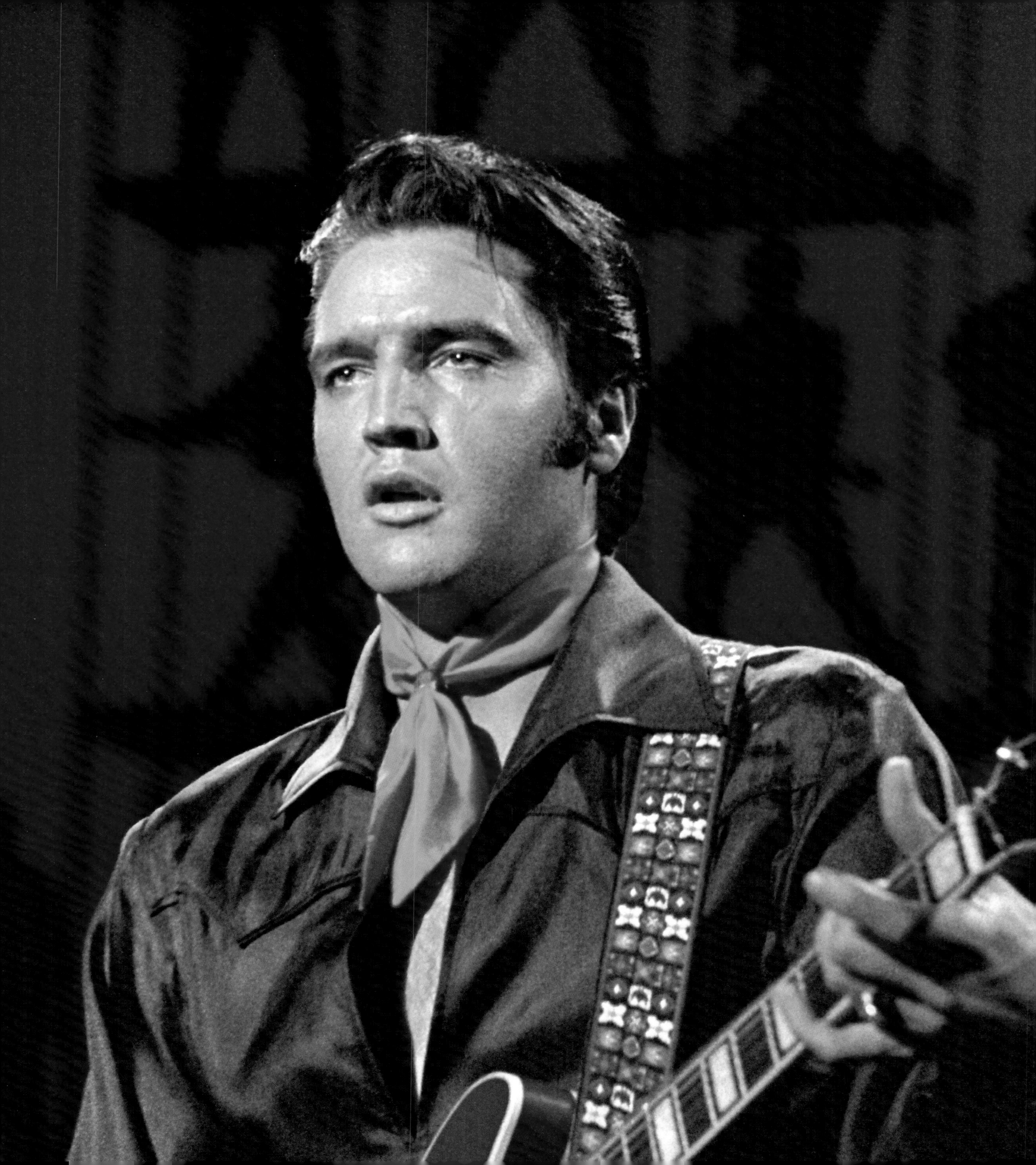

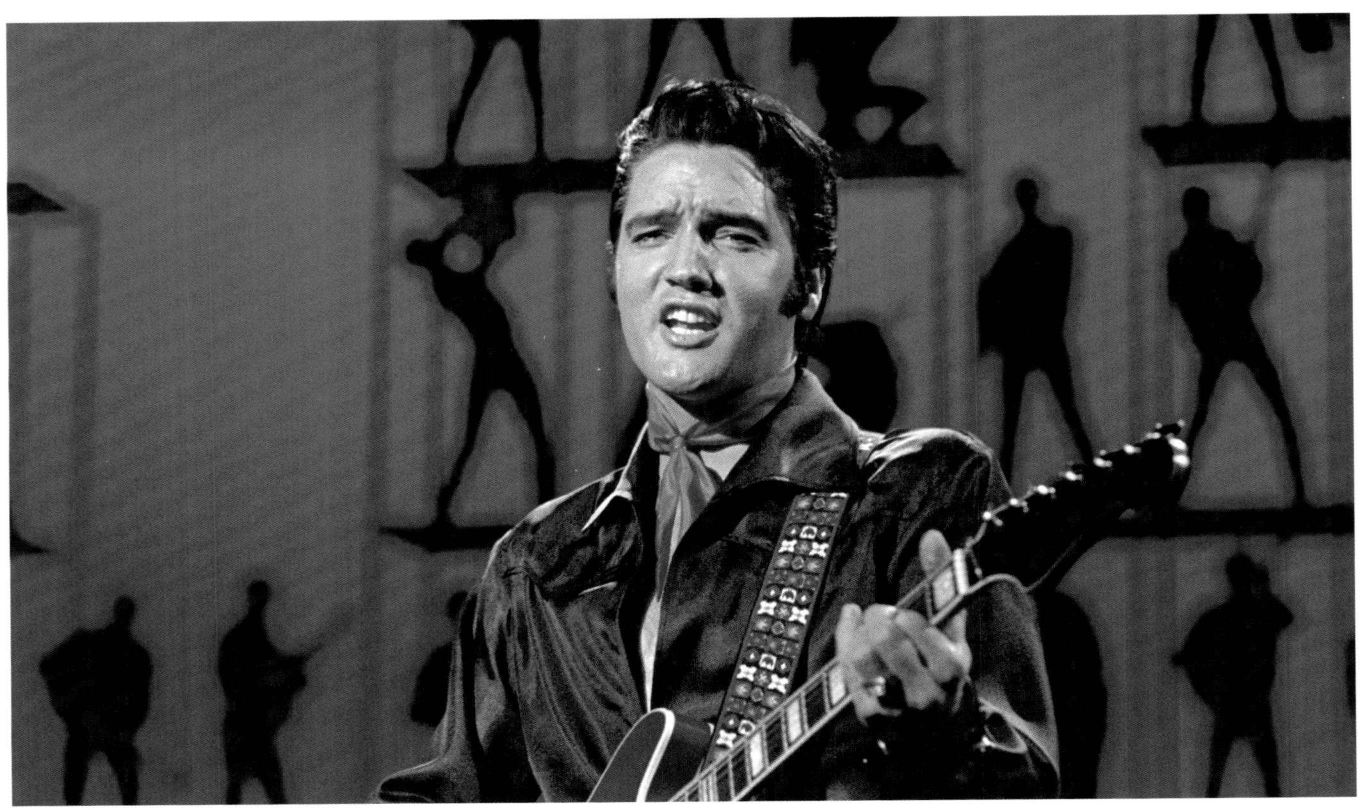

GOSPEL NUMBER:

The gospel segment is introduced by Elvis from his talk in the improv section where he explains how rock 'n' roll music sprang from gospel and rhythm and blues. Much to everyone's surprise on the special, Claude Thompson, who choreographed the Gospel segment of the show, cast himself in the solo that introduces the medley. The reason that I say 'surprised' is because Claude was very introverted and would be the last one to put himself in the spotlight. No one could have interpreted "Sometimes I Feel Like a Motherless Child" better than Claude.

When Claude choreographed the Gospel segment, it required a lot of staging from Elvis who became concerned about having to move and sing the lyrics to the medley at the same time. With his backup singers, the much respected Blossoms (Jean King, Fanita James and Darlene Love) singing live to track, Elvis asked if it would be possible to lip-sync the words and I told him that would be a big mistake. When we were at Western Recorders earlier doing the pre-record for the soundtrack, we had Elvis put the vocals on all the songs so it would help him memorize the lyrics.

At first Elvis agreed to try to sing the words live, but when it came to the actual taping of the medley, he changed his mind at the last minute and insisted he wanted to lip sync. I could only push so far. In my opinion, whenever any artist chooses to lip sync, the real 'emotion' is never there like when they sing live, especially when you're working with an artist like Elvis.

Elvis with The Blossoms: Jean King, Fanita James, and Darlene Love

"Elvis could be shy and introverted, but when it came to gospel music he opened up."

— DARLENE LOVE, The Blossoms

"People would be shocked to know how hard he worked on this special."
— *JAIME ROGERS, Choreography*

BORDELLO:

His next stop is walking into temptation, a house of ill repute. He rejects the older, experienced prostitutes waiting for their customers and his eyes go to a young girl with long blonde hair, actress Susan Henning, who represented 'innocence'. They spot each other, moving closer and closer, meeting up at the exact moment the house is raided by the vice squad. The guitar man jumps out of the window to avoid being arrested and finds himself on the road again. He continues his search for fame and fortune. The story is a framework for Elvis to sing a medley of songs.

All of a sudden, word got out that "Binder's shooting something really risqué on Stage 4" and we became the instant center of attention. The NBC censor assigned to the special immediately determined that the actresses, playing the part of the prostitutes, were dressed in costumes showing too much cleavage and insisted they be covered up. Bill Belew got a lot of black netting and with his costumers covered the girls' cleavage with the material in front of the entire crew.

While this was going on I heard rumors that even with the girls covered up the sponsors were considering taking the entire scene out of the final show. Upon hearing this, I gathered Alfred di Scipio, the Singer Sewing Executive, Farlan Myers of J. Walter Thompson and NBC executives, Don Van Atta, Dick Loeb, and Tom Kuhn along with the NBC censor and told them that I wanted them all to look at the set carefully. If they had any more objections to the girls' costumes, the set, including the brass bed in the center of the stage, or the other props, now was the time to speak up. Not one of them said a word.

I then asked for their guarantee that when I finished shooting the production number it would not be removed from the final cut. There was not one objection and that was the end of that. Or so I thought.

Earlier, Dick Loeb, a friend of mine and one of the NBC executives, coined the word 'bordello' when describing the set and mentioned it to the ad agency reps whose job it was to protect their client. Singer decided that the "Bordello" scene might offend the little ol' ladies in the Singer Sewing Centers across the country, and in spite of all their early promises and my objections, it was removed from the first broadcast but later re-inserted on following broadcasts. I heard later that the reason di Scipio and others all gave me their word to leave the scene in the show was because they were afraid I would walk off the show. And once the "bordello' scene was forced out of the original broadcast; we lost the song "Let Yourself Go." What none of them knew was that I never had any intention of quitting even if they forced me to take the scene out.

"The special was a natural extension of all our talents coming together at the same time."

— CHRIS BEARD, Writer

"When we first met with Steve he told us all they want is an Elvis Christmas Special and we said, "What do you need us for then?"

— ALLAN BLYE, Writer

Top far left: Susan Henning with Elvis in the Bordello Scene

GUITAR MAN JOURNEY:

Elvis, playing the part of the guitar man, makes his first stop at an amusement park boardwalk and gets into a fight with Big Boss Man, played by Buddy Arett abusing his girlfriend. This leads to the karate dance number where Elvis has to fight the Big Boss Man and his entire gang to defend her honor. Barbara Burgess played the part of the girlfriend.

Because I love to see and work with professional dancers, I decided to hire 35 of them and two of my favorite choreographers who would form two separate dance companies for the "Elvis" special: Claude Thompson and Jaime Rogers who I had met in New York while directing "Hullabaloo." Having two choreographers whose styles were so different and giving them their own choice of the many dancers we auditioned, created a spirit of friendly competition that really worked for the show. Claude was to be responsible for the Gospel segment and Jaime the Guitar Man journey.

Jaime Rogers, who starred on Broadway in "Golden Boy" with Sammy Davis, Jr., was responsible for choreographing the very physical karate fight dance segment that showcased his skills as a soloist as well. I loved seeing Jaime dance because he had a really rough edge based on his growing up in Spanish Harlem; he was a ball of fire with his outgoing personality and energy.

The only time Elvis balked at wearing one of Bill Belew's costumes was in the "Guitar Man" segment of the show. On his journey from rags to riches, Bill designed a version of Elvis' famous gold suit used on his album cover "50,000,000 Elvis Fans Can't Be Wrong." When Bill started to dress Elvis in the gold jacket, Elvis insisted he talk to me first. "Steve," he said, "Please don't ask me to wear that jacket man, I hate it!" I explained to him the concept behind it, that it was simply to show one of the transitions from a humble guitar player being forced to start out his career performing in dives with a belly dancer to fancier clubs and eventually making it to the top and playing huge arenas. He then put the jacket on willingly and said, "Let's get this over with as soon as possible."

After all the various 'adventures,' the "Guitar Man" realizes that true happiness for him was home and his guitar. *I'll never be more than what I am...Wouldn't you know...I'm a swinging little Guitar Man.*

"My jewel kept falling out of my bellybutton and I remember Elvis patiently waiting, making cute little remarks between takes."

—TANYA LEMANI, Little Egypt

"When I designed the boxing ring, I wanted to show the crowd was all around him, breathing on him. Elvis had the animal quality – always prowling around the stage."

— GENE McAVOY, *Art Direction*

"Then I did the '68 Special with Elvis and I gotta tell ya man, I listened to that every once in a while, and I played my ass off on that thing."

—HAL BLAINE, *Drummer*

IF I CAN DREAM:

The Colonel, frustrated and angry because his Christmas show had turned into something completely different kept insisting that at least one Christmas song be included in the special. He thought that "I Believe," a hit for Frankie Laine years ago, would be perfect. I never understood why he felt "I Believe" was a Christmas song, but I knew at some point we had to come up with something to satisfy him. I don't think the Colonel really cared whether the special was a Christmas show or not. All he wanted was to keep his power over Elvis in front of people he considered 'outsiders' like myself. Every decision he made that I ignored was, in his mind, a slap in his face.

Elvis and I entered his little office at NBC next to Stage 4 and he was sitting behind his desk in obviously a foul mood. "Bindel," his favorite name for me, "it's been called to my attention that you're not planning to have a Christmas song in the show...Bindel, is that true?" I replied that I really hadn't completed the entire list of songs we were using and I didn't want to do a Christmas song that would be sung on every other Christmas show. Staring almost through me, he angrily replied, "Well Elvis wants a Christmas song in the show so we're going to do a Christmas song in the show." He turned his gaze to Elvis, and said, "Isn't that right Elvis?" I looked over at Elvis standing by my side. I was hoping he would speak up, but instead he looked like a little child with his head bowed into his chin and his hands crossed in front of his private parts. He mumbled, "That's right Colonel." I remember answering the Colonel by saying, "If that's what Elvis wants, I'll make sure we put a Christmas song in the show." He responded "Good, now that that's settled you boys can go back to work," and we walked out into the hallway. No sooner as we left his office and we were out of earshot of the two William Morris interns, Elvis jabbed me playfully in the ribs with his elbow and said, "Screw him!" And that was that.

It should be noted that Bobby Kennedy was assassinated while we were rehearsing at the Binder-Howe offices on June 6th. I remember, the television set was playing and we all stopped rehearsal to find out what all the commotion was about. We, like all Americans, were stunned, and I remember spending all night with Chris, Allan and Elvis talking about what had happened since Martin Luther King and John Kennedy were gunned down. And now with Bobby, we both wondered what was happening to our country.

Knowing that the closing song of the special had to make a personal statement about Elvis, and knowing that time to find it was running out, I asked Billy and Earl to go home and write a song that would express who Elvis was. An Elvis who was thrown into the spotlight that seemed to really care about the world around him. Our television 'family' came from all walks of life, all religions, all races, and had one thing in common. We worked in television and wanted to do the best job we knew how using the most powerful medium in the world to say something not only entertaining, but meaningful.

Earl and Billy promised me that they would give it a shot. Not long after, Earl Brown phoned me at home to tell me that he and Billy had written the song I requested and were anxious to play it for me. We agreed to meet an hour before taping started the next morning. When I arrived at the studio, Earl and Billy were already waiting for me. We went into the empty piano room in Elvis's suite and they proceeded to sing to me "If I Can Dream."

Billy played the upright piano and Earl sang, "If I Can Dream of a better land, where all my brothers walk hand in hand"...and it went on from there until the end of the song. I asked them to play it again, and by that time I was convinced that I had found my closing song. When Elvis arrived at the studio and walked into his large dressing room, I went up to him, and motioned for him to follow me into the other room. At the same time, the Colonel and his group of cronies held court in Elvis' large dressing room.

I asked Elvis to sit next to Billy on the piano bench while Earl sang the song to him. Elvis listened, but gave no reaction. He asked them to sing "If I Can Dream" two or three times more without letting on to us whether or not he liked the song. He just sat there listening. I could hear the Colonel's voice through the door shouting "Over my dead body" and "They're wasting valuable time in there." Elvis looked at me and said "I'll do it; I'll sing the song on the show."

Big Ballad

Music: Intro Big Ballad

INTRO TO BIG BALLAD

WE COME UP ON
A LARGE INTERNALLY LIT SLIGHTLY RAISED
CIRCULAR AREA. WHICH ENABLES US TO SHOOT
IN THE
AROUND.

INTO THE
AREA WALKS A SINGLE
FIGURE. HE STANDS CENTRE
STAGE, AND AS THE INTRODUCTION
MUSIC BUILDS THE CAMERA
SLOWLY MOVES IN TO ELVIS. WE
SHOOT VERY TIGHT THROUGHOUT
ENTIRE NUMBER. USING SUBDUED
CONTINUALLY CHANGING SUBTLE
LIGHTING EFFECTS.

And with that, I opened the door to the big room and quietly announced that we had our closing song. The Colonel, with Tom Diskin at his side, obviously didn't want another open confrontation since he knew that Elvis had already said yes. He was biting his stogie and fuming. RCA's Norm Racusin had the contract and pen in hand for Billy and Earl to sign away their publishing rights. At the moment, Billy graciously admitted Earl had really written the song by himself and erased his name from the lead sheet.

"I was by the camera when Elvis sang my song "If I Can Dream" and I was thinking, "God, is this as great as I think it is?"

—EARL BROWN, Lyrics & Vocal Arrangements

BIG BALLAD.

ORIGINAL BIG BALLAD.
(WORDS TO COME)

AT THE END OF
THE BALLAD WE
DISSOLVE THROUGH
FROM MEDIUM C.U
TO TIGHT CU. OF
ELVIS. HE LOOKS
straight ~~RIGHT~~ INTO CAMERA. ELVIS (WITH TWINKLE IN HIS EYE) NOW.

How did that grab you??

WE CUT TO A
WIDE SHOT
AS WE HEAR
THUNDEROUS "LIVE
FEEL" AUDIENCE APPLAUSE, CHEERS, SCREAMS,
REACTION. WE
SEE TIGHTLY PACKED
ELVIS FAN AUDIENCE
IN BLEACHERS, SURROUNDING
ELVIS ON THREE SIDES
AND RISING STEEPLY AWAY.
THE LIGHTING AND
GENERAL FEEL IS
RAW AND OF A LIVE
CONCERT. ELVIS
WAILS INTO
POWERHOUSE OPENING
OF "JAILHOUSE ROCK"

WE CAN SHOOT LIGHTS AND "CREEPY PEEPY" CAMERAS IF NESSESARY.

MUSIC CUE. "MEDLEY".

Chapter 6

The Arena

While preparing the special and going through hundreds of photographs of Elvis, I came across one of Elvis sitting on his Harley Davidson motorcycle dressed in leather and it reminded me of when I saw Marlon Brando in "The Wild Ones" movie. I showed the picture to Bill Belew and asked him if he could duplicate the outfit for Elvis for one of our segments. He told me that rather than copy the same store-bought clothes, he would like to design a special leather suit for Elvis to use in the show. I told him to go for it and we ended up using it twice, once in the Arena segment and then again in the improv segment. What neither of us thought about at the time was how it would be for Elvis under those extremely hot theatrical lights. That provoked Elvis saying: "Man this thing's hot I'm telling you" referring to his leather suit before singing "Love Me Tender" in the Arena segment of the show.

I mentioned earlier that I had to use one of the pre-built sets for the improv segment because the decision from the Colonel that I could recreate the dressing room jam sessions didn't happen until we were near the end of our production schedule. There was no time to build a new set from scratch and besides, Gene told me he had exhausted his budget for the scenery. What we used was the intimate 'boxing ring' set used for the Elvis medley of hit records called the Arena Segment.

Our plan from the very beginning was to use our full orchestra and background singers to play and sing live while Elvis sang a condensed version of Billy Goldenberg arrangements of Elvis' classic hit records like "Heartbreak Hotel," "Blue Suede Shoes," "Jailhouse Rock," "Can't Help Falling In Love," "Hound Dog," "All Shook Up," "Don't Be Cruel" and "Love Me Tender."

Though there were times when we were forced to stop and pick-up again, my intention was never to stop the recording tape and shoot the entire segment as if it were a live concert. I didn't even block my camera shots in advance, but felt strongly that I would instinctively know when to change camera angles as Elvis moved around the small boxing-ring type stage.

Since there would be no post-production special effects, I did all of my superimpositions and effects in the camera at the time we were taping. The arena segment to me was as important to the overall success of the production as the acoustic segment turned out to be. In that black leather suit, and under the hot lights, Elvis proved once again that there were no gimmicks associated to his voice and charisma in front of a live audience. I've heard others describe his performance as if watching a black panther in a cage. They weren't far off.

A first in variety television was the use of a hand-held camera in the special that I had to beg NBC sports to use for the arena and improv segments. I had seen the use of this small, mobile camera by watching NBC football when they first introduced it to the public. I knew immediately that this technical invention could free up directors from the large and cumbersome studio cameras and help to capture the intimacy of a performer in hand-held documentary style. I think it added a lot of excitement to both of those segments.

I was determined to capture the real Elvis and not the homogenized version that was being presented whenever he appeared on his earlier television appearances or in his movies. Ordinarily, and up to this time when a singer appeared on television, they would be asked to stand on a specific mark placed on the floor directly in front of them (called a t-mark) where the lighting director would have a key light on the singer's face and a backlight for the hair and shoulders, with one or two fill lights added.

The camera would be placed directly in front of the singer and if the director wanted the singer to move, another mark would be placed on the floor for the singer to walk to where it would be lit and shot exactly the same way. I didn't want to ask Elvis to go to any marks on the floor, so I asked John Freschi, our lighting director, to light the entire stage so Elvis could be freed up to go anywhere his instincts took him.

As far as I was concerned this was not going to be 'traditional television' but had to be an authentic rock 'n' roll concert. If his hair was mussed up and he was sweating profusely, so be it! If cameras or equipment, normally hidden from the television audiences view, was seen in the shot… who cared? Well, NBC and the Singer Company evidently cared a lot. The minute they saw the raw Elvis and sweat pouring down his face from the hot lights and leather suit, they asked me to either re-shoot or take those scenes out of the special. One NBC executive, Dick Loeb, actually commented to me, "You can actually see sweat stains on his shirt under his arm pits and you won't be able to show that on prime time television. You'll have to edit that out of the show." Thank God they didn't get their way.

When we started taping, Elvis was visibly nervous. He said to the audience, "It's been a long time baby!" and you could see he meant every word. I could actually see his hand shaking as he took hold of the microphone, but once he started singing and he felt the electricity in the room, he relaxed and metamorphosised into the Elvis that the world was waiting to see again. He had returned to his roots.

Chapter 7

Post-Special

When I went into editing and saw all the great improv segments, I said "This IS the show." I've got to get a lot of this material in." So when I finished editing I had completed a 90-minute version. I phoned Finkel and told him what I had done and did he think it would be possible to open up another 30-minutes of airtime. He laughed and promised he'd try but didn't really hold out any hope for that to happen. The show's sponsor, Singer, flatly refused and I was forced to remove what I considered to be the heart of the show, the improvisation segment. The 60-minute version that originally aired on NBC had only brief snippets of the improv used only as interstitial glue for the production segments.

On August 16th, I delivered all the masters and outtakes to NBC. A few days later, after the Colonel had seen a screening of the special, I was ordered into a meeting with Tom Sarnoff and Herb Schlosser (President of NBC at the time). When I walked through the glass door leading to Herb Schlosser's office, the Colonel was already sitting there leaning on his cane. During the entire meeting he never took his steel blue eyes off of me. I actually had the feeling he was trying to hypnotize me. Schlosser told me that the Colonel was extremely unhappy and called his attention to the fact that there was no Christmas song in the show. The Colonel informed him that he wouldn't allow NBC to air the show without one. Silence prevailed while they waited for an answer from me. With the full knowledge that I never shot any Christmas songs except Elvis singing "Blue Christmas" in one of the improv segments, I said that I could pull out one of the other songs in the show and put "Blue Christmas" in its place. The entire time I spoke I was staring right back at the Colonel. The Colonel told Schlosser that he was satisfied with my solution since all he really cared about from the beginning was saving face. Ironically, a year later, on August 17th 1969, NBC rebroadcast "Elvis" and replaced "Blue Christmas" with "Tiger Man."

When I completed editing the 60-minute version of the show with my editors Wayne Kenworthy and Armond Poitras, I set up a screening for Elvis in one of NBC's small projection rooms. It was a dark room with about 15 theater seats. Elvis showed up with Jerry Schilling, Joe, Charlie, Lamar, Alan, Jerry Schilling and I invited a few key members of my staff. During the screening it was hard not to stare at Elvis to watch his reactions to the show. He appeared to me to be pretty relaxed and, on occasion, laughing at himself in the right spots.

When the lights went up, Elvis asked if he could see it again but this time without all the people in the room, except for me. I was sure he was holding back while they were there, and now wanted to tell me what he wanted taken out or changed before the show aired. All of my insecurities came to the surface. As soon as I finish my final edit on any project, I always fall into a funk. I guess it's because I'm so high while I'm directing, with all my adrenalin flowing, that when everything suddenly stops, I crash. I hate waiting to hear what other people, even the star, have to say about my work. There are times when I don't want to even look at my work. Some shows that I've produced and directed that I personally felt missed their mark have brought me great acclaim in the industry while others that I thought I did my best work in have been most criticized. All I ever cared about was the respect and love of the people I worked with.

I asked the tape operator to turn the speakers up to their maximum volume and to roll the tape for the second time. During the screening Elvis would lean over to me time and time again to say how much he loved what he was looking at. This time he wasn't holding back. His laughs were louder and his enthusiasm was contagious. It was like he couldn't believe his eyes. When it was over and the lights came up, he told me how proud he was of the show and how glad he was that he trusted me. Then he got in one of his quiet moods. I could tell that he was thinking hard. He told me that because of this new found 'freedom' (his exact word) that he experienced; he would never again make a movie or sing a song that he didn't believe in. I told him that as much as I wanted to believe him, I wasn't sure he was strong enough. I told him that the first thing he had to do was take control of his life, even if that meant breaking away from the Colonel.

"ELVIS" was first broadcast at 9:00PM on Tuesday, December 3rd, 1968. On December 4th, when the ratings were released, NBC reported that "ELVIS" captured 42% of the total viewing audience. It was the networks biggest rating victory for the entire year and the seasons #1 top rated show.

The 90-minute version of the special would not be seen by the public until after Elvis' death on November 20th, 1977, when NBC rushed to air a three-hour tribute special titled "Memories of Elvis" hosted by Ann-Margret which combined "Aloha From Hawaii" with the '68 Special. As the years passed by and by sheer accident, someone new at NBC, when told to retrieve the master tape of the special, grabbed the 90-minute version not realizing this was not the show that aired in '68. Truthfully, I thought they had erased it or destroyed it, but they obviously hadn't.

When Elvis opened in Las Vegas soon after, I went to see him and he was fantastic. I made an attempt to go backstage and say hello and congratulate him, but the Security Guard at the Hilton said he couldn't reach anyone when he phoned Elvis's dressing room to announce me. I always felt that the Colonel had put out the word right after the special aired, that I was persona non-grata and Elvis was never even told that I was downstairs

I have always considered the "ELVIS" special to be the last of a trilogy of specials I directed and produced that began with Leslie Uggums and then continued with Petula Clark. Had I not brought to the table an amazing group of talented artists to surround me, and had we not had a chance to experiment and nourish each other twice before working as a close family creatively on the other two specials, I don't think the "ELVIS" special would have achieved its iconic place in television history.

Sadly, in 2007 Claude Thompson and Bill Belew passed away. Then in January of 2008 Earl Brown followed. I remember writing Claude a thank you note immediately after the special aired. "Dear Claude," I wrote, "Of all the choreographers I have worked with I have never seen anybody achieve more love and respect for the people they work with. What I am more proud of is not the fact that we do shows together, but the fact that I know you as a human being. I hope our relationship goes on for many, many years." There are many times, even now, that I wish we had all stayed together for the remainder of our careers.

Chapter 8

Recording Sessions

Location:

WESTERN RECORDERS, BURBANK, CALIFORNIA

JUNE 20, 1968

Nothingville / Guitar Man (Part 1) (Guitar Man Section 1)

Let Yourself Go (Part 1) (Guitar Man Section 2)

Let Yourself Go (Part 1) (Female Vocal Overdub)

Flicker Routine / Let Yourself Go (Part 2)

Let Yourself Go (Part 3)

Alley Pickup (Guitar Man Section 3)

Let Yourself Go (Composite)

Guitar Man (Part 2 - Fast) (Escape Section 1)

Amusement Pier Music (Escape Section 2)

Big Boss Man (Escape Section 3)

It Hurts Me (Part 1) (Escape Section 4)

JUNE 21, 1968

Guitar Man (Part 2 - Slow) (Escape Section 1 Remake)

It Hurts Me (Part 2) (After Karate Section 1)

It Hurts Me (Composite)

Guitar Man (Part 3) / Little Egypt (After Karate Section 2)

Trouble / Guitar Man (Part 4) (After Karate Section 3)

Road Medley (Composite)

Sometimes I Feel Like A Motherless Child /
Where Could I Go But to The Lord /
Up Above My Head - Intro (Gospel Section 1)

JUNE 22, 1968

Up Above My Head / I Found That Light / Saved Intro (Gospel Section 2)

Saved (Part 1) / Preach For The Sky / Saved (Part 2) (Gospel Section 3)

Gospel Medley (Composite)

Trouble (Opening)

Guitar Man (Opening)

JUNE 23, 1968

Karate Musical Interlude (Instrumental)

The Scratch (Instrumental)

If I Can Dream

If I Can Dream (Dubdown to Rhythm Track)

Memories (Rhythm Track)

Let Yourself Go (Closing Instrumental)

A Little Less Conversation (Rhythm Track)

JUNE 24, 1968

Mono and Stereo Mixing Session

JUNE 24, 1968

Memories (Vocal Overdub)

A Little Less Conversation (Vocal Overdub)

Let's Forget About The Stars (not attempted)

Can You Find It In Your Heart (not attempted)

"Not Me" ("Truckstop Romance") (not attempted)

Musicians:

Guitar: Tommy Tedesco

Guitar: Michael Deasy

Guitar: Al Casey

Bass/Keyboards: Larry Knechtal

Bass: Charles Berghofer

Piano: Don Randi

Drums: Hal Blaine

Percussion: John Cyr

Percussion: Elliot Franks

Bongos: Frank DeVito

Harmonica: Tommy Morgan

Keyboard: Bob Alberti

Keyboard: Tommy Wolfe

Backup Vocalists:

The Blossoms: Darlene Love, Jean King, Fanita James

Julie Rinker, B.J. Baker, Frank Howren, Bill Lee, Gene Merlino, Thurl Ravenscroft, Bill Brown, Joe Eich, Elaine Back, Dean Parker, Jack Gruberman, Sally Stevens, Jackie Ward, Ronald Hicklin, Tom Bahler, and Mitch Gordon

Orchestra:

Conductor: Billy Goldenberg

Arrangers: Billy Goldenberg; Jack Elliot

Violin: Leonard Atkins; Leonard Malarsky; Sidney Sharp; Thelma Beach; Marvin Limonick; Joseph Stepansky; Alexander Murray; Ambrose Russo

Cello: Eleanor Saltkin; Paul Bergstrom; Christine Walevska; Emmett Sargeant; Richard Noel; Frank Rosolino; Ernest Tack

Trombone: Francis Howard

Trumpet: Oliver Mitchell, John Audino, Manny Stevens, Anthony Terran

Saxophone: Anthony Ortega; Peter Christlies; John Kelso; Gene Cipriano

French Horn: Dick Perrisi; William Hinshaw

Location:

ELVIS PRESLEY'S DRESSING ROOM, NBC / BURBANK STUDIO, BURBANK, CALIFORNIA

JUNE 24, 1968

I Got A Woman

Blue Moon / Young Love / (The Sun Is Shining)

Oh Happy Day

When It Rains It Really Pours

Blue Christmas

Are You Lonesome Tonight? / That's My Desire

That's When Your Heartaches Begin

Love Me

When My Blue Moon Turns To Gold Again

Blue Christmas

Santa Claus Is Back In Town

JUNE 25, 1968

Danny Boy

Baby What You Want Me To Do

Love Me

Tiger Man

Santa Claus Is Back In Town

Lawdy Miss Clawdy

One Night

Blue Christmas

Baby What You Want Me To Do

When My Blue Moon Turns To Gold Again

Blue Moon Of Kentucky

Musicians:

Acoustic Guitar / Electric Guitar: Elvis Presley

Acoustic Guitar / Electric Guitar: Scotty Moore

Acoustic Guitar: Charles Hodge

Percussion: D.J. Fontana

Percussion: Alan Fortas

Tambourine: Lance Legault

Location:

NBC / BURBANK STUDIO, BURBANK, CALIFORNIA

JUNE 25, 1968

Press Conference Held

Location:

NBC / BURBANK STUDIO, BURBANK, CALIFORNIA

JUNE 27, 1968 (VIDEOTAPED)

Big Boss Man - Amusement Pier Part 1

It Hurts Me - Amusement Pier Part 2

It Hurts Me - Amusement Pier Part 2 pickups

It Hurts Me - partial overdub

JUNE 27, 1968 - Warm-Up Rehearsal*

That's All Right

Heartbreak Hotel

Love Me

Baby What You Want Me to Do

Blue Suede Shoes

Lawdy Miss Clawdy

Are You Lonesome Tonight?

Santa Claus Is Back In Town

When My Blue Moon Turns To Gold Again

One Night

Memories

Musicians:

Acoustic Guitar / Electric Guitar: Elvis Presley

Acoustic Guitar / Electric Guitar: Scotty Moore

Acoustic Guitar: Charles Hodge

Percussion: D.J. Fontana

Percussion: Alan Fortas

* It is presumed that this rehearsal was not recorded on audio or videotape

JUNE 27, 1968 (VIDEOTAPED) - 6:00 PM Improv Segment

That's All Right

Heartbreak Hotel

Love Me

Baby What You Want Me To Do

Blue Suede Shoes

Baby What You Want Me To Do

Lawdy Miss Clawdy

Are You Lonesome Tonight?

When My Blue Moon Turns To Gold Again

Blue Christmas

Trying To Get To You

One Night

Baby What You Want Me To Do

One Night

Memories (singing to pre-recorded rhythm track)

JUNE 27, 1968 (VIDEOTAPED) - 8:00 PM Improv Segment

Heartbreak Hotel

Baby What You Want Me To Do

Introductions

That's All Right

Are You Lonesome Tonight?

Baby What You Want Me To Do

Blue Suede Shoes

One Night

Love Me

Trying To Get To You

Lawdy Miss Clawdy

Santa Claus Is Back In Town

Blue Christmas

Tiger Man

When My Blue Moon Turns To Gold Again

Memories (singing to pre-recorded rhythm track)

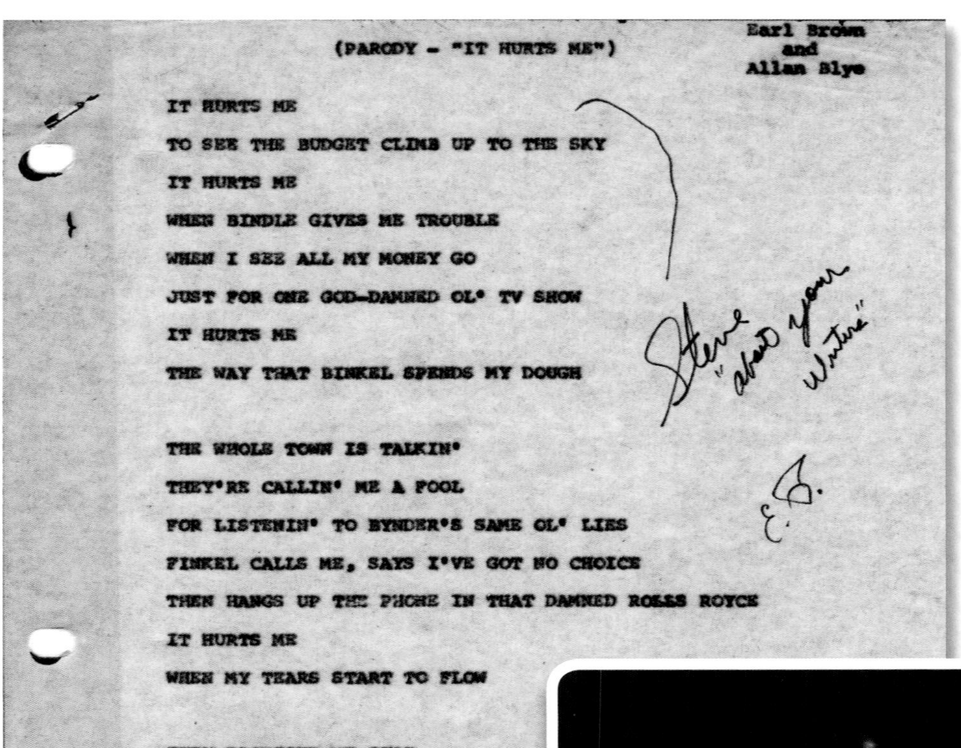

(PARODY - "IT HURTS ME")

Earl Brown
and
Allan Blye

IT HURTS ME
TO SEE THE BUDGET CLIMB UP TO THE SKY
IT HURTS ME
WHEN BINDLE GIVES ME TROUBLE
WHEN I SEE ALL MY MONEY GO
JUST FOR ONE GOD-DAMNED OL' TV SHOW
IT HURTS ME
THE WAY THAT BINKEL SPENDS MY DOUGH

THE WHOLE TOWN IS TALKIN'
THEY'RE CALLIN' ME A FOOL
FOR LISTENIN' TO BYNDER'S SAME OL' LIES
FINKEL CALLS ME, SAYS I'VE GOT NO CHOICE
THEN HANGS UP THE PHONE IN THAT DAMNED ROLLS ROYCE
IT HURTS ME
WHEN MY TEARS START TO FLOW

THEY PROMISED ME SURE
IF I WOULD GIVE IN
THAT I WOULD - THAT I WOULD
NEVER GO WRONG
BUT TELL ME THE TRUTH
IS IT TOO MUCH TO ASK
FOR ONE LOUSY, TIRED OL'
CHRISTMAS SONG...?

June 26, 1968: Elvis taking a break during the special to celebrate Colonel Parker's birthday party with photo of Executive Producer Bob "Napolean" Finkle and to sing the parody of "It Hurts Me" to the NBC executives.

Musicians:

Acoustic Guitar / Electric Guitar: Elvis Presley

Acoustic Guitar / Electric Guitar: Scotty Moore

Acoustic Guitar: Charles Hodge

Percussion: D.J. Fontana

Percussion: Alan Fortas

Tambourine: Lance Legault

JUNE 28, 1968 (VIDEOTAPED)

Sometimes I Feel Like A Motherless Child / Where Could I Go But To The Lord /Up Above My Head

Up Above My Head / Saved

Saved Part 2 pickups

Saved Part 3 pickups

Let Yourself Go - Bordello Part 1

Let Yourself Go - Bordello Part 2

Let Yourself Go - Bordello Part 3

Bordello insert

Bordello Part 2 - no Elvis

JUNE 29, 1968 (VIDEOTAPED) - 6:00 PM Arena Segment

Heartbreak Hotel (Incomplete)

One Night (Incomplete)

Heartbreak Hotel

Hound Dog

All Shook Up

Can't Help Falling In Love

Jailhouse Rock

Don't Be Cruel

Blue Suede Shoes

Love Me Tender

Trouble / Guitar Man*

Baby What You Want Me To Do

If I Can Dream (lip-synched performance)

JUNE 29, 1968 (VIDEOTAPED) - 8:00 PM Arena Segment

Heartbreak Hotel

Hound Dog

All Shook Up

Can't Help Falling In Love

Jailhouse Rock

Don't Be Cruel

Blue Suede Shoes

Love Me Tender

Trouble (False Start)*

Trouble (False Start)*

Trouble / Guitar Man (Incomplete)*

Trouble / Guitar Man (Reprise)*

Trouble / Guitar Man (Reprise)*

If I Can Dream (lip-synched performance)

Musicians:

Electric Guitar: Elvis Presley

Guitar: Tommy Tedesco

Guitar: Michael Deasy

Guitar: Al Casey

Bass / Keyboards: Larry Knechtal

Bass: Charles Berghofer

Piano: Don Randi

Drums: Hal Blaine

Percussion: John Cyr

Percussion: Elliot Franks

Bongos: Frank DeVito

Harmonica: Tommy Morgan

*singing to pre-recorded rhythm track

Backup Vocalists:

Julie Rinker, B.J. Baker, Frank Howren, Bill Lee, Gene Merlino, Thurl Ravenscroft, Bill Brown, Joe Eich, Elaine Back, Dean Parker, Jack Gruberman, Sally Stevens, Jackie Ward, Ronald Hicklin, Tom Bahler, and Mitch Gordon

JUNE 30, 1968 (VIDEOTAPED)

Nothingville - Road #1

Guitar Man (Road #1 Vocal Overdub)

Guitar Man (Road #2 Vocal Overdub)

Guitar Man (Road #3 Vocal Overdub)

Huh-huh-huh Promo

If I Can Dream (Vocal Overdub)

Trouble (Opening Overdub) / **Guitar Man** (Opening Playback)

Guitar Man (Alley, Vocal Overdub)

Little Egypt / Trouble (Nightclub, Vocal Overdub)

Trouble (Discotheque, Vocal Overdub)

Trouble (Supper Club Vocal Overdub)

Closing Credits

Orchestra:

Conductor: Billy Goldenberg

Arrangers: Billy Goldenberg; Jack Elliot

Violin: Leonard Atkins; Leonard Malarsky; Sidney Sharp; Thelma Beach; Marvin Limonick; Joseph Stepansky; Alexander Murray; Ambrose Russo

Cello: Eleanor Saltkin; Paul Bergstrom; Christine Walevska; Emmett Sargeant; Richard Noel; Frank Rosolino; Ernest Tack

Trombone: Francis Howard

Trumpet: Oliver Mitchell, John Audino, Manny Stevens, Anthony Terran

Saxophone: Anthony Ortega; Peter Christlies; John Kelso; Gene Cipriano

French Horn: Dick Perrisi; William Hinshaw

June 23, 1968 at Western Recorders with guitarists Tommy Tedesco (left) and Michael Deasy

168

SUMMARY LAYOUT SHEET
Page 1

DECEMBER 1968 - VICTOR LP RELEASE
(Ships - Immediately)

LPM-4088 "ELVIS" LIST CATEGORY - LPM - $4.79
Side 1
WPRM-8051 "NEW ORTHOPHONIC" HIGH FIDELITY P8S-1391 ELVIS.DEC 1968release

** 1- TROUBLE TP3-1008 3:26 * WPA1-8030 Elvis Presley Music Inc., BMI
(Leiber-Stoller)
GUITAR MAN TP3-1008 * WPA1-8047 Vector Music Corp., BMI
2- LAWDY, MISS CLAWDY TP3-1008* WPA1-8031 Venice Music Inc., BMI
(Lloyd Price)
BABY, WHAT YOU WANT ME TO DO* WPA1-8032 Conrad Music, BMI
(Reed)
DIALOGUE TP3-1008
Medley: TP3-1008
a. HEARTBREAK HOTEL * WPA1-8083 a.Tree Music, BMI
(Axton-Durden-Presley) *
b. HOUND DOG * WPA1-8034 b.Elvis Presley ## Music Inc., & Lion Pub. Co. Inc. BMI
(Leiber-Stoller)
c. ALL SHOOK UP TP3-1008 * WPA1-8035 c.Elvis Presley Music Inc.,& Travis Music Co., BMI
(Blackwell-Preley) *
CAN'T HELP FALLING IN LOVE * WPA1-8036 d.Gladys Music Inc., ASCAP
(Weiss-Peretti-Creatore)
JAILHOUSE ROCK TP3-1008* WPA1-3037 e.Elvis Presley Music Inc.,BMI
(Leiber-Stoller)
DIALOGUE f.Elvis Presley Music Inc., BMI
LOVE ME TENDER TP3-1008
(Presley-Matson
(from the Original Sound Track Of his NBC-TV SPECIAL)
Elvis Presley
*TAPES PURCHASED FROM NBC ##J.Leiber & M. Stoller, BMI
RECORDING DATES NOT AVAILABLE

**Recorded in stereo

TP3-1008 ELVIS.....APRIL 1969 RELEASE

LISTING
DEC 9 1968
ORIGINAL COPY

169

SUMMARY LAYOUT SHEET
Page 2

DECEMBER 1968VICTOR LP RELEASE
(Ships-Immediately) LIST CATEGORY - LPM -$4.79

LPM-4088 "ELVIS" P8S-1391 ELVIS..DEC 1968 RELEASE
Side 2
WRPM-8052

** 1-DIALOGUE
WHERE COULD I GO BUT TO THE LORD* WPA1-8039 Affiliated Music Enterprises,Inc.,BMI
TP3-1008
(J.B.Coats)
UP ABOVE MY HEAD * WPA1-8040 Gladys Music Inc., ASCAP
(W.Earl Brown) TP3-1008
SAVED
(Leiber-Stoller) 7:25 * WPA1-8041 Progressive Music Pub. Co. Inc., & Trio
2-DIALOGUE TP3-1008 * WPA1-8042 BIBO Music Pub., Inc. ASCAP
+BLUE CHRISTMAS
(Hayes-Johnson)
DIALOGUE * WPA1-8043 Elvis Presley Music Inc., & Travis Music Co., BMI
ONE NIGHT
(Bartholomew-King) 5:37
#3-MEMORIES TP3-1008 3:18 * WPA1-8044 Gladys Music Inc., ASCAP
(Strange-Davis

** 4-Medley: TP3-1008 6:42 * WPA1-8045 a. Gladys Music Inc., ASCAP
a. NOTHINTVILLE
(Strange-Davis)
DIALOGUE TP3-1008 * WPA1-8046 b. Ludix Pub. Co. & Conrad Music, BMI
b. BIG BOSS MAN
(Smith-Dixon) * WPA1-8047 c. Vector Music Corp., BMI
c. Guitar Man
(Jerry Hubbard) * WPA1-8048 d. Elvis Presley Music Inc., & Trio
d. LITTLE EGYPT
(Leiber-Stoller) * WPA1-8030 Music Co. Inc., & Progressive Music Pub.
e. TROUBLE
(Leiber-Stoller) * WPA1-8047 Co. Inc., BMI
e. Elvis Presley Music Inc., BMI
f. GUITAR MAN
(Jerry Hubbard)
*5-IF I CAN DREAM TP3-1008 3:16 * WPA1-8029 f. Vector Music Corp., BMI
(W.Earl Brown) 5. Gladys Music Inc.,ASCAP

TP3-1008 ELVIS
(from the Original Soundtrack of his NBC-TV Special
Elvis Presley

*TAPES PURCHASED FROM NBC
RECORDING DATES NOT AVAILABLE

LISTING
DEC 9 1968
ORIGINAL COPY

**Recorded in stereo

+ CPL8-3699
☆ CPL1-1349
CPL2-4031

FINAL

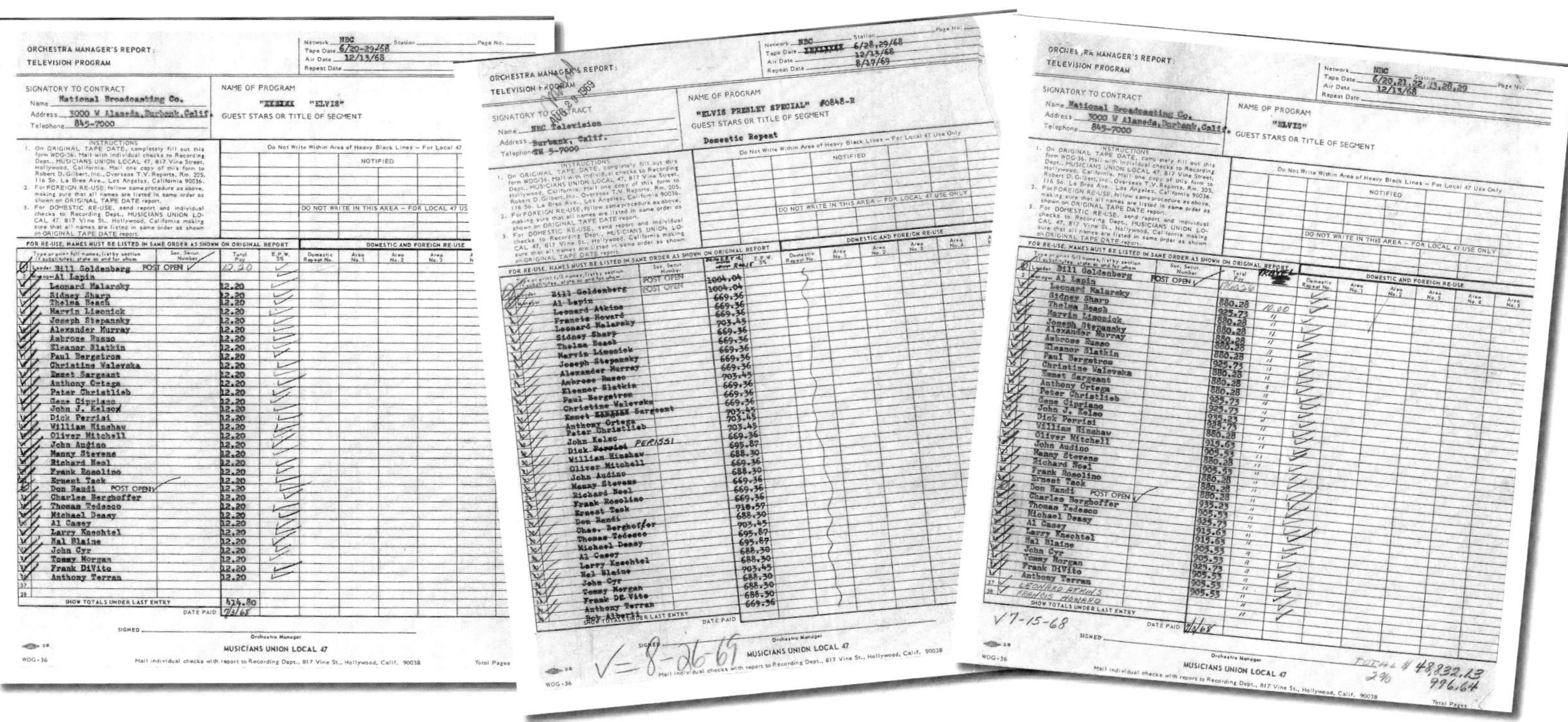

ORCHESTRA MANAGER'S REPORT:
TELEVISION PROGRAM

Network NBC
Tape Date 6/20-29/68
Air Date 12/13/68

SIGNATORY TO CONTRACT
Name National Broadcasting Co.
Address 3000 W Alameda, Burbank, Calif.
Telephone 845-7000

NAME OF PROGRAM "ELVIS"

Name	Total Pay
Leader Bill Goldenberg POST OPEN	12.20
Manager Al Lapin	
Leonard Malarsky	12.20
Sidney Sharp	12.20
Thelma Beach	12.20
Marvin Limonick	12.20
Joseph Stepansky	12.20
Alexander Murray	12.20
Ambrose Russo	12.20
Eleanor Slatkin	12.20
Paul Bergstrom	12.20
Christine Walevska	12.20
Emmet Sargeant	12.20
Anthony Ortega	12.20
Peter Christlieb	12.20
Gene Cipriano	12.20
John J. Kelson	12.20
Dick Perrisi	12.20
William Hinshaw	12.20
Oliver Mitchell	12.20
John Audino	12.20
Manny Stevens	12.20
Richard Neol	12.20
Frank Rosolino	12.20
Ernest Tack	12.20
Don Randi POST OPEN	12.20
Charles Berghoffer	12.20
Thomas Tedesco	12.20
Michael Deasy	12.20
Al Casey	12.20
Larry Knechtel	12.20
Hal Blaine	12.20
John Cyr	12.20
Tommy Morgan	12.20
Frank DiVito	12.20
Anthony Terran	12.20
SHOW TOTALS UNDER LAST ENTRY	414.80
DATE PAID	7/3/68

MUSICIANS UNION LOCAL 47
Mail individual checks with report to Recording Dept., 817 Vine St., Hollywood, Calif. 90038
WDG-36

ORCHESTRA MANAGER'S REPORT:
TELEVISION PROGRAM
AUG 29 1969

Network NBC
Tape Date 6/28,29/68
Air Date 12/13/68
Repeat Date 8/17/69

SIGNATORY TO CONTRACT
Name NBC Television
Address Burbank, Calif.
Telephone TH 5-7000

NAME OF PROGRAM "ELVIS PRESLEY SPECIAL" #0848-R
GUEST STARS OR TITLE OF SEGMENT Domestic Repeat

Name	Soc. Secur. Number	Total Pay
Bill Goldenberg	POST OPEN	1004.04
Al Lapin	POST OPEN	1004.04
Leonard Atkins		669.36
Francis Howard		669.36
Leonard Malarsky		703.45
Sidney Sharp		669.36
Thelma Beach		669.36
Marvin Limonick		669.36
Joseph Stepansky		669.36
Alexander Murray		669.36
Ambrose Russo		703.45
Eleanor Slatkin		669.36
Paul Bergstrom		669.36
Christine Walevska		669.36
Emmet Sargeant		703.45
Anthony Ortega		703.45
Peter Christlieb		703.45
John Kelso		669.36
Dick Perissi		695.87
William Hinshaw		688.30
Oliver Mitchell		669.36
John Audino		688.30
Manny Stevens		669.36
Richard Noel		669.36
Frank Rosolino		669.36
Ernest Tack		710.57
Don Randi		688.30
Chas. Berghoffer		703.45
Thomas Tedesco		695.87
Michael Deasy		695.87
Al Casey		688.30
Larry Knechtel		688.30
Hal Blaine		703.45
John Cyr		688.30
Tommy Morgan		688.30
Frank DeVito		688.30
Anthony Terran		669.36
Bob Alberti		

V= 8-26-69

MUSICIANS UNION LOCAL 47
Mail individual checks with report to Recording Dept., 817 Vine St., Hollywood, Calif. 90038
WDG-36

ORCHESTRA MANAGER'S REPORT:
TELEVISION PROGRAM

Network NBC
Tape Date 6/20,21,22,23,28,29
Air Date 12/13/68

SIGNATORY TO CONTRACT
Name National Broadcasting Co.
Address 3000 W Alameda, Burbank, Calif.
Telephone 845-7000

NAME OF PROGRAM "ELVIS"

Names: Leader Bill Goldenberg POST OPEN; Manager Al Lapin; Leonard Malarsky; Sidney Sharp; Thelma Beach; Marvin Limonick; Joseph Stepansky; Alexander Murray; Ambrose Russo; Eleanor Slatkin; Paul Bergstrom; Christine Walevska; Emmet Sargeant; Anthony Ortega; Peter Christlieb; Gene Cipriano; John J. Kelso; Dick Perrisi; William Hinshaw; Oliver Mitchell; John Audino; Manny Stevens; Richard Noel; Frank Rosolino; Ernest Tack; Don Randi POST OPEN; Charles Berghoffer; Thomas Tedesco; Michael Deasy; Al Casey; Larry Knechtel; Hal Blaine; John Cyr; Tommy Morgan; Frank DiVito; Anthony Terran; Leonard Atkins; Francis Howard

Total Pay: 880.28, 925.73, 880.28, 880.28, 880.28, 880.28, 880.28, 925.73, 880.28, 880.28, 880.28, 925.73, 925.73, 935.23, 925.73, 880.28, 915.63, 905.53, 880.28, 905.53, 880.28, 880.28, 880.28, 935.23, 905.53, 925.73, 915.63, 915.63, 905.53, 905.53, 925.73, 905.53, 905.53, 905.53

TRAVEL 10.00

V7-15-68
DATE PAID 7/3/68

MUSICIANS UNION LOCAL 47
Mail individual checks with report to Recording Dept., 817 Vine St., Hollywood, Calif. 90038
WDG-36

TOTAL $48,832.13
2% 976.64

About the Author

Steve Binder

Steve Binder has a long and distinguished career in television, film and music. An Emmy winner and multiple-nominee for both the Emmy and Golden Globe Awards, Steve has been guest speaker on two separate occasions at the prestigious William Paley Center (formerly named the Museum of Television & Radio) in both Los Angeles and New York where an evening was devoted to his work in the entertainment industry including winning the Ace Award for directing "Diana Ross in Central Park."

Robert Hilburn, music critic of the Los Angeles Times, wrote about Binder's feature film, The T.A.M.I. Show as, "One of the top ten all time great rock'n roll films." This 1963 historical film starred: The Rolling Stones, James Brown, Marvin Gaye, The Beach Boys, The Supremes, Chuck Berry, The Miracles, Gerry and the Pacemakers, Leslie Gore and Jan & Dean.

Steve was keynote speaker to a standing room only audience at the Hall Of Fame Museum of Rock'n Roll in Cleveland, Ohio. His subject was his highly acclaimed 1968 "Elvis" NBC television special what TV Guide called "The second greatest musical moment in television history next to the Beatles debut on Ed Sullivan." "This legendary special offered not only an unplugged session years before the term became the vogue, but yielded the finest music of Elvis's career" accorded noted rock critic and historian Greil Marcus.

Steve is currently an active member of the Directors Guild of America, The Producers Guild of America, The Caucus, and serves on the Board of Governors of the Academy of Television Arts & Sciences representing the Directors peer group. He attended the University of Southern California where he serves as an adjunct professor in the film and television school and received an Honorary Doctorate of Humane Letters from Columbia College Hollywood.

"More than anything else, Steve Binder has remained successful living with his philosophy: "Whatever you do in life, do it with passion...passion is everything."

68 at 40 Reunites: March 14, 2008

Left to right: Priscilla Presley, Steve Binder, and Bones Howe at the Paley Film Festival celebrating the 40th Anniversary of the Elvis Special.

Left to right: Steve Binder, Bones Howe, Allan Blye, Lance Legault, and Chris Bearde also attending the Paley Film Festival.

'ELVIS'

Elvis Presley in a musical special. Executive producer Bob Finkel. Producer-director Steve Binder. Writers Allan Blye, Chris Beard. Musical production Bones Howe. Musical direction and arrangements William Goldenberg. Special lyrics and vocal arrangements Earl Brown. Choreography Jamie Rogers, Claude Thompson. NBC, Tuesday, 9 p.m.

The Elvis hour on NBC was virtually a one-man show with the star doing most of his numbers on a small square stage surrounded by a studio audience which had some screamers in it. But according to executive producer Bob Finkel, none of them were hand-picked. They just simply loved Elvis.

Although he didn't indulge in the dynamic physical gyrations which made him so controversial that we saw only the top half of him on an Ed Sullivan Show many years ago, Elvis still generates considerable heat with his singing.

His repertoire included many of his recorded hits such as "Hound Dog," "Jailhouse Rock" and "Love Me Tender." Producer-director Steve Binder employed lots of camera closeups and two-camera superimposed shots, which were effective, except for those closeups showing Elvis sweating. I don't think many viewers care to see singers sweat on TV.

Moving away from the small stage and studio audience, Elvis did two impressive production numbers. One was a gospel song with dancers and singers; the other opened on a carnival midway and progressed from his singing in a joint to better-class night-clubs.

The show closed with him in a white suit standing in front of the huge lit letters spelling E-L-V-I-S which opened the proceedings, and he sang "If I Can Dream."

Except for TV runs of his old movies, this marked Elvis' first TV appearance since he did a guest shot on a Frank Sinatra special in 1960, so it was an event in that sense and Elvis managed to sustain the hour very well.

"Thank you, good night."
—Elvis